AF292564

Also in the
Wellcome Collection
Anthology series:

Thirst: In Search of Freshwater

The Coming of Age

Notes on Getting Older

Foreword by
Sharon Blackie

First published in Great Britain in 2026 by Wellcome Collection

183 Euston Road
London NW1 2BE
www.wellcomecollection.org

Curators: Shamita Sharmacharja and Ruth Horry
Editor: Ellen Johl
Copy-editor: Patrick Taylor
Proofreader: Kate Brook
Designer: Bret Syfert
Suminagashi Textures: Margot Lombaert
Producer: Petra Essing
Typefaces: Pyros, Dia & Libre Baskervile
Distributed by Thames & Hudson
Printed and bound in Great Britain by Pureprint Group
The moral rights of the authors have been asserted.

A catalogue record for this book is available from the British Library.

ISBN 978-1-9998090-6-5 MP-7726.2/3500/03/2026/BS

Contents

Foreword: The Old Woman
Who Lives in the Land
Sharon Blackie   9

Life on Mars
Angela Saini   23

The Science of Why We Age
Venki Ramakrishnan   35

Ageing in the Past
Molly Conisbee   53

The Fight to Get Old
Travis Alabanza   69

Ageing and Care
Lynne Segal   81

Who Gets to Age Well?
Pragya Agarwal
95

Rethinking Ageing for
the Twenty-First Century
Andrew J. Scott
113

Dare We Grow Old?
Vicky Spratt
131

Ageing Across the Globe
Sweta Rajan-Rankin
143

Disability, and Other Denials
Tom Shakespeare
157

Endnotes
176

About the Authors
182

About the Exhibition
188

Foreword

The Old Woman Who Lives in the Land

by **Sharon Blackie**

When I lived for four years on the far south-western fringes of the Isle of Lewis in the Western Isles, just over a decade ago, my very best friend was an old woman made of rock. Lewisian gneiss, to be precise: one of the hardest and most ancient rocks on the planet. I'd recently staggered across the bewildering threshold that is menopause, and I was beginning to look around me for contemporary role models who might point the way to a rich and meaningful elderhood. There weren't any. So I turned instead to my friend made of rock, to see what timeless geological wisdom she might have to offer.

I stumbled across that old woman by accident while exploring a cleverly hidden, low-slung section of the storm-tossed shoreline on which we were so precariously perched: a remarkable location on which I bestowed the rather unremarkable name of The Rocky Place. It consisted of a vast expanse of smooth, slabbed rock: a multilayered pink, brown and grey carpet which gently sloped down to a cluster of smaller rocks, coated with emerald-green algae, onto which the Atlantic Ocean continually crashed. The Rocky Place's boundary with the grassy headland above was defined by a long, sharply chiselled escarpment, perhaps the height of two average people.

   The Old Woman Who Lives in the Land

A jutting protrusion of rock from the cliff face offered up the rough-hewn silhouette of a decidedly haggish old woman, slightly larger than human height, staring out to sea.

Steeped in myth and folklore as I am, I instantly claimed her as the Cailleach: the archetypal Old Woman of the World in the Gaelic tradition. Because in our oldest cosmologies, it wasn't a white-bearded father-god up in the sky who made and shaped this world: it was a giant old woman who has been with us down all the long ages, since the beginning of time. 'When I was a young lass, the ocean was a forest, full of trees,' she declares in some of the stories about her. Other stories tell us that she has a penchant for staring out to sea to watch for the return of her long-lost husband, who's sometimes simply called the Bodach (the 'old man') and other times identified as Manannán Mac Lir, an old Celtic god who makes his home in the ocean. Just around the corner from this Cailleach rock, I discovered a vast, flat mattress of gneiss tightly wedged into an alcove in the escarpment. It looked like a giant sofa, fit for any super-sized Flintstone. I called it the Cailleach's Bed, and sometimes I would sleep there to celebrate the return of the stars at the end of those long, too-light Hebridean summers.

The Gasker light would flash slowly out to sea to the south of me, and the Flannan Isles lighthouse would blink to its own unique rhythm, farther north.

I've spent some considerable time wondering why that specific rock, that specific mythic character, haunted me so when I was 50 years old. I'd say now that this old Cailleach rock taught me everything I then needed to know about strength and endurance, about standing your ground in the face of the everlasting storms that batter their way through a woman's life. We might imagine that myths are about the gods, but they're really about us. About the weightiness of the human condition and, in the context of my own particular story at the time, about coming to terms with the innumerable challenges of growing old.

The Cailleach's favoured landscapes are always wild and rocky places, and there are other sites throughout the islands and mainland Scotland where the shapes of specific rocks, mountains or ranges represent the usually recumbent silhouette of this old goddess who is so deeply identified with the land. The best known of them is the Isle of Lewis's 'Sleeping Beauty' configuration, which in Gaelic is called Cailleach na Mointeach: the old woman of the moors; she can be seen on the far south-eastern horizon from the Callanish stone circle.

In most stories about her, the Cailleach also has a fearsome and decidedly seasonal character: she's associated with winter, the old season, the wildest and most challenging half of the year. In some folklore, particularly in the Western Highlands, she appears in conjunction with her younger sister Bride, who supplants her early in the year and presides over spring and summer – until Samhain comes around and the Cailleach rises up to rule again. The many folk tales in which she mimics the cycles of death and re-birth in nature, then, show us just how closely this mythical old woman was identified with the natural world. A good few stories tell of her ability to repeatedly renew herself, becoming young again after she has grown very old. In one such tale, the Cailleach rejuvenates herself every hundred years by bathing in Loch Bà on the Isle of Mull at Là Bealltainn, May Day – but only if she manages to get down to the water before the sun has risen and before a single bird has sung or a dog barked.

It has always seemed to me that these stories of a divine old woman who is so profoundly entangled with the seasons and cycles of nature can help women learn to dance with the ever-shifting rhythms of our own lives, too. They help us to navigate the turbulence of the flow, and remind us that to age well is to fall into step with the pulses of the land. Several stories also portray the Cailleach as a guardian of the balance of the natural world that she reflects and represents – especially when it comes to the need to protect it against humans. And so one tale tells of her preventing Donald Cameron, a hunter in Lochaber, from killing members of a herd of female deer which she was driving. Seeing him raise his gun to shoot, she called out to him: 'You are too hard on my hinds, Donald! You must not be so hard on them!' Donald, quick-witted and clearly no fool, responded immediately, saying: 'I have never killed a hind where I could find a stag.' He allowed the hinds to pass, from that time took only the occasional stag, and the Cailleach never bothered him again.

British folklore offers us an abundance of ancient hags who are immanent in the land, who reflect the cycles of the seasons, or who preside over the weather and can summon storms – and who can talk to birds and animals. These mythic old women are presented as spirits of the wild Earth itself, in stories which originated in eras when the landscape was symbolised as a wom-

 The Old Woman Who Lives in the Land

an's body: caves as wombs, rivers as veins, hills as breasts … Our rugged giantesses were builders and shapers too, constructing roads and mountain ranges, flooding valleys to create deep lakes abundant with energy and life. So an old folk tale tells us that a giantess from North Wales once decided to build a bridge across the Menai Strait from Caernarfon to the island of Anglesey. She took herself off to search for suitable boulders, pressing on over high mountains and along deep valleys, until finally she arrived at a place called Cwmdwythwch in what is now the Eryri National Park (formerly Snowdonia). There, she gathered up the corners of her apron and loaded a great pile of boulders into it. But just as she came down the north side of Moel Eilio on her journey back to the coast, the giantess slipped and slid, and her great heels gouged out two streams which flowed ever afterwards down the side of the mountain. She landed on her backside with an emphatic thump – and to this day, that place is known as Gafl y Widdan: the Witch's Lap. Undeterred, she staggered to her feet, gathered up her apronful of stones again and continued on her way. But she didn't get very far before the cord of her apron broke, and her bundle full of boulders tumbled to the ground. The pile of rocks lay there for a very long time and became known as Barclodiad y Gawres: the Giantess's Apronful.

England has its share of these powerful old women too, and a giantess called Bell was once known to have lived with her husband, Wade, in the vast and rugged landscape of the North York Moors. Wade built Mulgrave Castle as a home for himself, and Bell built Pickering Castle, which stood a good eighteen miles away, directly across the moors. Bell had a giant cow, and it was her daily duty to milk the animal. At times, especially in the inclement climate of that bleak landscape, it was difficult even for a giantess to cope with that chore: the moors were riddled with deep and dangerous bogs, and the weather could be simply atrocious. The only thing that might conceivably ease Bell's often-challenging task was a good track – and she did so long for a footpath along which she could walk in comfort and safety to milk her cow. One day, she mentioned this to Wade, and it was decided that they should construct a road between the two castles.

Just like our intrepid Welsh giantess, Bell gathered up great piles of stones from the beaches and from the moors, using her massive apron to carry them. Wade used Bell's stones to build the causeway, making a base of the larger ones

    The Old Woman Who Lives in the Land

and finishing with ever-smaller ones until eventually a fine, smooth surface was produced. Any surplus or unsuitable stones, such as the very large ones, were carried away again by Bell in her capacious apron, but one morning her apron strings broke, and she lost an entire load of stones – the equivalent of twenty carts full – and they're still there today as a high hill near the causeway. At various points between Whitby and Pickering, there remain many scatterings of isolated stones; these were others which fell from her apron during her long, hard work. Bell's road on the North York Moors does still exist, but as is often the way of such things, it is now named after her husband: Wade's Causeway.

There are so many stories about wise and powerful older women scattered throughout European myth and folklore, and I've written about them extensively and collected them together in two of my recent books – but really, why should they matter to us today? For me, it's because the old women in these old stories are, quite simply, forces of nature. There are no distant, ethereal star-goddesses here; there are no dowager fairy queens, reluctant to defile themselves with the mess of physical incarnation. Our old women are the stony heart of the mountain, rooted and immanent in the living land itself. They remind us that it's not our destiny, no matter how inconvenient the overculture might find ageing women to be, to just sit quietly and invisibly in a corner and wait to die. They show us how we might live after menopause has stripped away everything we once thought defined us. They teach us how to stand firm and stay grounded in the face of inevitable death. These gigantic older women are as tough as the rocks they carry and the wild, windswept land that they embody. They show us that to be elder is not always to be fragile and frail: it is also to be strong and enduring, hard and fierce and wild. To be elder is to be powerful and to stay the course: always to remain fully alive and engaged, through all the long years till our work here is done. Now, so many old ways of perceiving the world have disappeared from everyday life – but the stories of these old women have not. They've lived on, just as the age-old women in them have lived on, through all the long ages of the Earth.

The powerful elder women who stand against the exploitation of animals and the land, who are the guardians and protectors of the natural world, offer us a smorgasbord of strong role models, too – inspiring us to stand our ground

     The Old Woman Who Lives in the Land

and fight for nature in the face of ecological catastrophe. In these troubled times, we women need to dig deep to uncover our inner Cailleach: to defend the integrity of the wild places of this world and the other-than-humans who share it with us. These keepers of ancestral wisdom are our allies in this work, teaching us that we are the land and the land is us. Once, they were revered – and if our native mythology includes strong and powerful elder women, then their stories can inspire us to insist that we should be taken seriously, that we should have our voices heard too – not only for our own sakes, but for the sake of the planet itself.

I don't live in the Western Isles any more, and that rocky old Cailleach is little more now than a distant friend who still sometimes finds her way into my dreams. But here in the wind-soaked North Pennines of England, I hear her still in the wild, hag-like shriek of the heron down on the banks of the river which slivers through the lush green fields below my house. I see her in the shadowy comings and goings of the hares up on the high common, the preferred shape for feisty old northern witches to shift into so that no one might poke a nose into their dark, mysterious business. There's a wide, stony track running up over the fell which might conceivably have been built by a giantess-sister of Bell. Wherever you live, there'll be an Old Woman who lives in the land. I'd encourage you to make her acquaintance: she has some age-old wisdom to proffer. The steady, solid wisdom of the land – of the bedrock on which the foundations of all our lives are built. When she was a young lass, the ocean was a forest, full of trees. She's seen so many changes, that Old Woman, and she knows what we so often fail to understand: change isn't only inevitable, it's indispensable. So that new shapes and patterns are always in the process of becoming, and the end of all things might be held at bay for a few long ages more.

     The Old Woman Who Lives in the Land

Life on Mars

by **Angela Saini**

It was after she retired that my mother's career began.

For decades, she had worked alongside my father in one family business after another. It was long, hard, often thankless work. A woman who had come to Britain with next to nothing, perfecting her English in fits and starts, she built up her confidence over the years. When my father decided to retire early and sell up the last business they owned together, around the same time that my sisters and I left home to go to college, she found herself suddenly unmoored. I thought she might take up a gentle hobby. It was with some surprise, when I came to visit my parents one day, that I discovered she was out *at work*. While my father stayed at home, tending his beloved garden and doing the housework, my mother had become a social worker. Within a decade, she was the head of the facility where she worked, proudly carrying the keys to the building in her handbag. By then, she was in her seventies.

She had finally proven something to herself. What's more, it was only in this phase of her life that it had become possible.

In the fourth and final book of *Tetrabiblos* – the ancient Greek astronomer Ptolemy's fantastical treatise explaining the meaning of the planets and the stars – the different phases of life are compared to celestial bodies in the Solar System. For the ancients, ageing was the most dramatic of metamorphoses, at least in the mortal realm, dispatching each of us across the heavens within our own lifespans. According to Ptolemy, the Moon represented innocent babyhood; Mercury and Venus were vibrant, tumultuous youth; the Sun was the sensible start of adulthood; Mars was gentler middle age; and Jupiter and Saturn represented the quiet reflection of the final years.

Ptolemy had men in mind when he wrote *Tetrabiblos*. Women are often feared or disparaged in ancient Greek literature, treated as a breed apart. But women's transformations are, of course, no less profound than men's. I wonder, in fact, if the changes experienced by women may run deeper.

In India, from where my parents migrated in the 1970s, old age and menopause are seen by many as a welcome liberation from the burdens of their childbearing years and the pressures of living up to society's rigid expectations. The cultural distinctions between men and women dissipate. Women are able to access public spaces more freely, to speak their minds more openly. The demure, passive housewife is often expected to grow into a strident, dominant mother-in-law. In extended family households – still common in Asia – older women have far more power than both the younger women and the younger men. In the last remaining matrilineal societies in some parts of India, older women are the literal matriarchs, the keepers of their family lineages and property.

There are endless stories of older super-women. Roshni Devi Sangwan from the northern Indian state of Haryana started weightlifting at the age of 68 and is now, in her seventies, a viral sensation for her ability to perform deadlifts of 70 kilograms. In the southern state of Tamil Nadu, the oldest president of any village council is Veerammal Amma, a grandmother in her late eighties. In Kerala, Meenakshi Raghavan, also in her eighties, is believed to be the oldest woman in the world practising the weapon-wielding, high-skill Indian martial art, Kalaripayattu.

When we think about our lives, our minds often linger on the period after childhood and before old age, as though those years are the only ones that define us. When people consider what it means to be a woman, their responses frequently revolve around the experiences of childbirth and motherhood. But what about the lives we lead on

　　　　　　　　　　　　　　　　Life on Mars

either side of that window? There are profound lessons to be learned from the people we are when our bodies are in their transitional states, on the Moon and on Saturn, to take Ptolemy's metaphor. These are the times when we don't experience the physical effects of sex difference at their strongest, nor society's gendered demands at their tightest. It is in early childhood, then later in old age, that we are given the most latitude to be just ourselves.

Gender matters hardly at all when we're born. We start our lives as babies almost indistinguishable from one another. Sexual difference has very little meaning in the first decade of a child's life, the stage that Ptolemy compared to the Moon. Before puberty, there are no average differences in strength between girls and boys. Our voices sound the same. Were it not for the gendered norms we impose on them, the ways in which we cut their hair, the clothes we make them wear, the toys we hand them, it would be almost impossible to tell very young boys and girls apart. It is in that early part of their lives that girls have the licence to be tomboys if they want, to play with whoever they choose. It was in primary school, I recall, that we all played football together. The older we grew, the more separate the girls became from the boys.

At puberty, masculinity and femininity begin to feel more noticeable. Bodies become more easily distinguishable by sex. It shouldn't surprise us that adolescents find these years such a shock. They are being carried at light speed to their next destination, one in which nothing is the same, including themselves. The outside world's attitudes towards us shift perceptibly the second we are no longer little children. I was twelve, I recall, when a boy first patted me on the bum in the street while I was out shopping with my best friend. My friend laughed and told me to forget about it. We had, I realised in that moment, transitioned into a new phase of our lives. We had landed on Mercury, and here, the rules were different. Our bodies were no longer fully our own.

In *Dreams of Trespass*, her memoir of growing up in one of Morocco's last harems in the 1940s, the sociologist Fatima Mernissi captured poignantly the ebbing away of freedom she experienced as she transitioned from being a child – like any other child, boy or girl – to being a woman. Trapped inside the high walls of the harem, women were expected to accept their lot as a consequence of what was believed to be the natural order. There were more than a few echoes of ancient Athens in her account, a place where society's gender norms similarly manifested in a literal separation of men and women. The ideal Athenian woman was a devoted mother and wife, quietly confined to the *oikos*, the home. The domain of men was the *polis*, the public space.

It is telling that Mernissi wrote her memoir not from the perspective of herself as an adult, but by imagining herself again as a child. It was as a child that she could see most clearly the hypocrisies of a system that some of the women in her family had grown to accept as inescapable tradition. As a child, she was fully equal to others her own age. As a woman, she was not. In the end, Mernissi did trespass across the threshold of the harem, enjoying a life of study, travel and freedom that her mother had privately hoped her daughter would have. The harems disappeared, creating an avenue for her to live life by her own rules. It is hard not to imagine that it was the child's voice within her that propelled her forward.

I recall my surprise many years ago when my mother – then middle-aged – told me that she still felt like a young girl inside. I simply couldn't reconcile the person I knew, the person sitting in front of me, with the person she imagined herself to be. I wonder now if it was also the child's voice inside her that inspired her to start a new job in her later years. Her ambitions and dreams were always there, waiting for their moment.

In her book *Flash Count Diary*, the American writer Darcey Steinke describes evocatively the sensation of freedom that came with ageing and the menopause, precisely because it allowed her to wriggle free of society's gendered demands. 'I don't possess the strong female signifiers I once did,' she writes. A little like in early childhood, the physical distinctions between women and men are less noticeable in older age. As much as we might resist it, the body loses its definition. Hairs sometimes sprout on the chin; the voice becomes gruffer. For men, too, their faces and bodies become softer. Masculinity wanes. As we grow older, the visible signs of our gender begin to melt away.

Steinke doesn't regard this as a loss, though. The second time she was inadvertently called 'sir' by a stranger, she didn't stop to correct them. She realised that the only way to fully prevent it from happening again was to put on more make-up and wear more feminine clothes. But she found that she no longer had any interest in propping up her gendered appearance this way. She allowed her femininity to fray.

Age had made her androgynous, and that was fine.

Gender is not a static quantity, then. It isn't handed to us at birth, after which its meaning stays the same forever. It is mediated both by how much importance society puts on it, and also – as we see – by our *age*. There are periods in our lives when gender matters more to how we live and how we feel about ourselves. But there are other periods when it matters far less, and occasionally not at all. Age is the underappreciated factor that shuttles us back and forth between these gendered and ungendered states. In older age, we can escape the tight noose of a gendered society, not because society is different – but because *we* are.

As women, though, we are often taught to fear that change. In the 1960s, the American gynaecologist Robert Wilson terrified a generation of women with the claim that 'all post-menopausal women are castrates'. Hormone replacement treatments were marketed on the promise that they would give husbands back their wives as they remembered (and preferred) them: young, juicy and plump. Even now, entire industries exist to help us cling to that narrow period of womanhood for as long as possible, through high-tech cosmetic enhancements and biological interventions, pumping us with fillers and vitamins. The goal is to be frozen in an artificial youth, feminine forever.

What do we lose when we insist on staying young? In his book *What to Expect When You're Dead*, the philologist Robert Garland surveyed the world's oldest cultures and their attitudes to ageing, death and the afterlife. What set the ancients apart from us in the present was their proximity to death, he writes, living as they did in a time before modern medicine, when mortality rates were high. This didn't make them any less fearful of death, but it did nurture a healthy fatalism. *Carpe diem*. The unerring presence of the dead was the most pressing reminder that one should seize the day. As the ancients knew, age is not something that can be outpaced. Lost in the illusory promise of a future without wrinkles, we forget that, just as Ptolemy wrote, every stage of life in fact transports us to new worlds.

I myself am about to land on Mars. I can see it on the horizon, the Sun receding into the distance. What a relief it is to be leaving behind that previous stage of my life: the slow climb up the career ladder, the exhausting early years of

                                    Life on Mars

parenthood, the precarious uncertainty of finding the right home. On Mars, I can rest a little, reflect a while. I am taken more seriously here. I command a respect that I didn't have when I was younger. I don't have to worry so much about how I look, or what people think of me. In hushed tones, my friends and I admit what an underrated joy we find middle age to be.

Seeing what my mother has achieved in her later years, the carefree abandon with which she now lives her life, I look at the years to come with a sense of hope, too. It is not that I blithely welcome ageing, that I don't worry about the prospect of physical or mental decline (I dab cream under my eyes religiously every night). But I have learned to see old age for what it might offer rather than for what it will take away. I look forward to giving even less of a damn than I give now, of going entirely unnoticed as I walk down the street, of speaking my mind as loudly as possible.

If relinquishing the straitjacket of gender is the price to pay for growing older, for travelling to Jupiter or Saturn, is it so bad? Might it be even better than life on Mars?

The Science of Why We Age

by **Venki Ramakrishnan**

Cells in our body die and are replaced all the time – and we don't even notice it.

Paradoxically, at the moment of our death, most of our cells are still alive, and entire organs remain functional. As humans, we fear death, but it is a particular kind of death: the loss of our ability to function as a conscious individual. We are only aware of our mortality and the prospect of death because we have evolved a brain that has consciousness – self-awareness – as well as language to communicate the idea.

For most of humanity's existence, there was nothing we could do about ageing and death. But today, biologists have made major advances in understanding ageing, and for the first time provide the promise of tackling the many causes of ageing to allow us to live longer, healthier lives.

But why do we age at all? One answer is that there is wear and tear and a general increase in entropy, which causes the system to wind down. However, this does not explain the enormous variation in lifespans. There are insects like the mayfly, which in its final form lives only for a day, and other creatures like the Galapagos tortoise, the bowhead whale or the Greenland shark that live for a very long time, in the latter case for as long as over 400 years.

The Science of Why We Age

You might think that this is because a biological program in each species specifies how long it can live, but this isn't so. Rather, evolution mainly tries to optimise our 'fitness' – the term biologists use for maximising the chances of each organism being able to successfully pass on its genes. In real life, resources are limited. In order to optimise fitness, a choice has to be made between allocating resources to growth and reproduction versus maintenance and repair, needed for longevity.

On average, the larger the animal, the longer its lifespan. Whales, sharks, giant tortoises and elephants all live longer than mice or rats. It makes no evolutionary sense for a small animal to spend limited resources to age slowly if it is going to be eaten or starve to death fairly quickly. Small animals spend their resources to mature and reproduce quickly, thereby increasing their chances of raising offspring before they die. This is also why animals that can fly, like bats and birds, and so forage widely and escape predators, generally live much longer than animals of a similar weight that are land-bound. There are some curious exceptions to this – like us! Humans live almost twice as long as would be expected given our weight. Of course, our life expectancy has doubled in the last hundred years or so because of improvements in public health and medicine.

So most evolutionary biologists believe that ageing is not programmed, but simply a consequence of optimising for fitness given limited resources. But what about genes that affect ageing? There are mutations in worms that can double their lifespan. Even in humans, studies on identical twins suggest that there is up to 25 per cent heritability in lifespan. The genes that affect lifespan were not selected for longevity, but rather for advantages early in life, making us more likely to pass on our genes – for example, to prevent cancer, or to promote rapid growth early in life – and ageing is an unintended later consequence. In fact, these genes are selected for even if they are detrimental later in life after our reproductive window has passed. Those mutant worms cannot compete with normal worms, showing that the increased longevity comes at a cost to fitness.

The longest-lived human on record was Jeanne Calment, who lived to be 122 years old. No one has lived past 120 in the thirty years since Calment died. According to Thomas Perls, a professor at Boston University School of Medicine who studies centenarians, the number of people who live to be over 100 has grown as a result of advances in medicine, but the number who live to over 110 has not significantly changed, suggesting that about 110 years is the limit of the natural lifespan of our species as selected for by evolution.

Could we exceed it, however, by altering our natural biology? In principle, there is no physical or chemical law saying that our maximum lifespan has to be 120 years. But there is also no physical law saying we can't colonise Mars – it's just that there are enormous difficulties in both cases. Moreover, it's not clear whether we can drastically alter our fundamental processes while retaining the very characteristics that make us human.

Although lifespans can vary enormously, the underlying biology in all species, especially among mammals, is so similar that the mechanisms of ageing are very much the same. Roughly speaking, ageing can be thought of as the accumulation of changes and damage to our body that causes gradual dysfunction over time. When this dysfunction results in the failure of a critical system such that the body can no longer operate as a coherent whole, it leads to death.

Scientists have grouped these changes into

'hallmarks' of ageing. When the level of a hallmark goes up, ageing accelerates, and when its level is reduced, ageing slows down. These hallmarks encompass every level of complexity from the molecular to the cellular and tissue levels. They span the entire gamut: from DNA damage, modification of DNA and telomere loss, to the loss of control over protein production and quality control, loss of regulation of the processes that control nutrient sensing, mitochondrial damage, increase in the number of senescent cells, depletion of stem cells (which are responsible for regenerating all our tissues), as well as communication between cells. Viewed this way, ageing encompasses practically all of biology. These different hallmarks of ageing are very much interconnected, so ageing is a complex, multifactorial process. The end results are outward manifestations, such as frailty, loss of mobility and cognition, and many of the morbidities of old age.

Each of these aspects of ageing provides a potential anti-ageing therapeutic target – and some of them seem to me to be more promising than others.

Caloric restriction is shown to slow down ageing and improve the health of older animals in many species. In such a regimen, an animal

   The Science of Why We Age

is fed the bare minimum of calories and essential nutrients to keep it alive indefinitely. Caloric restriction is difficult for humans to practise. Among its reported side effects are reduced wound healing, being more prone to infection, loss of muscle mass, feeling cold and a loss of libido. The alternative is to use drugs that mimic caloric restriction. We know that caloric restriction affects a number of pathways, most notably the TOR pathway (often referred to as mTOR), a major pathway in the cell that controls growth in response to nutrients in the environment. Inhibiting the TOR pathway by drugs turns off or slows down the synthesis of new proteins but also turns on autophagy, a process for recycling defective components in the cell. One such inhibitor is the drug rapamycin, which was originally discovered as an anti-fungal compound. Studies on animals have shown that rapamycin reproduces many of the effects of caloric restriction, including an extension of about 20–30 per cent in lifespan. This has led to great optimism among some researchers that rapamycin or its analogues can be used to combat ageing.

Other drugs that fall into this class are metformin, which is widely used to treat type 2 diabetes, and GLP-1 agonists, which are prescribed for weight loss and appetite suppression to morbidly obese people (including diabetics who are obese).

However, none of these drugs is a panacea yet. Rapamycin is an approved drug for immunosuppression to prevent organ transplant rejection. Although its effects on the immune system are complex, it is known to increase the risk of infections, slow wound healing and in some cases increase the risk of diabetes. Proponents of rapamycin argue that in lower doses, one can get the anti-ageing benefits of rapamycin without the side effects, and there are some studies that support this contention. However, long-term studies on its efficacy in healthy individuals are still needed.

Similarly, metformin is undoubtedly beneficial for diabetics. But despite its popularity with celebrities and even many scientists, its efficacy in healthy individuals is controversial, and properly controlled long-term studies will be needed to establish its utility and safety for treating age-related morbidities. And GLP-1 drugs have, among other side effects, the loss of muscle mass which would add to the frailty of older individuals.

A second class of drugs are based on attacking senescent cells. When cells undergo stress

　　　　　The Science of Why We Age

such as infection or DNA damage, they can commit suicide in a process called apoptosis, or they can go into a state called senescence, in which they no longer have their normal function, cannot divide, and secrete an array of inflammatory compounds that signal to the immune system to destroy them. There are good reasons for the evolution of senescent cells: a cell with damaged DNA is a potential cancer risk that can destroy the entire individual. Far better to destroy such a cell, and sending it into senescence provides a signal not just to destroy it but also to deal with the causes of damage at the site.

Senescent cells are therefore useful throughout our lives. They even play a role in the development of the embryo. As we grow older, however, cells undergo more stress and damage, and we accumulate far more senescent cells than our system can cope with. These cells produce a system-wide inflammation that in turn causes more tissue damage and the production of even more senescent cells.

Scientists have found that using specific chemicals to target senescent cells for destruction has ameliorated many of the symptoms of ageing in older mice. As a result, there are a number of 'senolytic' drugs that are being clinically evaluated. But in order to avoid affecting normal cells, such drugs need to be highly specific for senescent cells. Since senescent cells play an important biological function, it is important that we can control the extent to which they are destroyed.

A third class of drugs that may be developed in the future are based on results from parabiosis, an experiment in which an older and younger animal are joined together and their circulatory systems connected. In these experiments, the older animal benefits from the blood of the young animal, and vice versa, the young animal suffers from the blood of the older one. This shows that there are factors in blood that change with age, some of which might be beneficial and others that might be harmful. Blood contains hundreds of factors, so there exists a large research enterprise to identify factors that affect ageing, and then determine what they do and how they might be used to attack ageing. This is a long-term area of research, but it has not prevented both individuals and companies from trying to perform blood transfusions of plasma from young donors to rich, older individuals (mostly men!).

Our body breaks down the food we eat into basic building blocks from which we make all the essential molecules of life. As we grow older, our ability to make certain key molecules declines. In some cases, these molecules control a large number of chemical processes in the body, and a reduced level means that our metabolism may no longer be optimal. This has led to the idea that supplementing our diet with the immediate building blocks of important molecules can raise their level to what they were when we were young. Using this type of approach, scientists advocated dietary supplements of molecules that were reported to improve the health of mitochondria, the organelles in our cells that are the centres of energy production. More recently, there has been a lot of interest in precursors of the molecule NAD (nicotinamide adenine dinucleotide), which plays a central role in energy metabolism as well as in many other reactions. Some early studies are promising but again, longer-term, controlled studies will be needed to show that they are both effective and safe.

Perhaps the most exciting – but also the most challenging – approach to combat ageing is the idea of cellular reprogramming. Every cell in our body is descended from a single cell, the fertilised egg. As the egg divides, each cell in the embryo retains the ability to eventually develop into any cell type, whether it is a neuron, a skin cell or one of the cells of the immune system. These are called pluripotent stem cells. But as the embryo develops, the cells become specialised stem cells which can only regenerate their particular tissue types. Normally, the process never goes backwards. However, the ageing clock is re-set naturally every generation: every child starts at age zero. A child born to a 40-year-old woman is not twenty years older than one born to a 20-year-old woman.

The birth of a child arises from the sperm and egg, which are descended from germ cells that are better protected against damage and also undergo stringent selection to ensure that the resultant offspring is as free of defects as possible. However, nearly seventy years ago, John Gurdon showed that you could take the nucleus from the skin cell of an adult frog and grow an entirely new frog from it – a clone of the original animal. The new frog did not live a shorter life because it had originated from an older cell. So the process of development from a fertilised egg to the final collection of specialised cells that forms a fully grown baby can be reversed in some situations.

About twenty years ago, Shinya Yamanaka showed that just turning on four genes in a ful-

   The Science of Why We Age

ly differentiated cell (like a skin cell), now called Yamanaka factors, could turn it back into a pluripotent stem cell. Scientists are now asking whether this could be used to reverse ageing. But turning our cells into pluripotent stem cells would not be great: not only would it be a cancer risk, but our tissues would lose their identity. However, if it were possible to turn on these factors for a brief period, then we could turn back the clock and have cells revert to an earlier stage without losing their identity. This kind of experiment has been shown to improve the health of older mice, but so far it has not extended their lifespan.

The methods used to turn on these factors in mice are not easily adaptable to humans, though. There are enormous technical challenges in delivering these factors throughout tissues of interest in a controlled manner that is safe over the long term. But if it worked, it could be one of the few ways of partially reversing ageing, rather than merely slowing it down. The brain, however, which regenerates very little, remains a huge problem for these types of approaches.

With all of these therapeutics to possibly slow down or reverse ageing, a general stumbling block is whether or not ageing is considered a disease. Some scientists argue that, because many of the diseases of old age – such as cancer, cardio-vascular disease, diabetes and neurodegenerative diseases – have ageing as one of their biggest risk factors, ageing itself should be considered a disease. Others, including the WHO and the FDA, have not classified ageing as a disease, on the grounds that it is both ubiquitous and inevitable. This raises a problem for therapeutics, which depend on clinical trials.

The usual way to monitor whether an intervention has an effect on ageing is to measure lifespan via mortality. But this would take an unreasonably long time. As anyone who has been to a school reunion knows, people age at different rates. Scientists have developed various markers of ageing which are better indicators of someone's 'biological' age in the sense they can more accurately predict decline and death than someone's chronological age. The most common of these are specific patterns of methyl groups that modify our DNA. However, there are many other markers, such as the collection of factors in our blood or inappropriate sugar groups that are added to our proteins. We need to agree on a set of markers to measure ageing to measure the effectiveness of various therapeutics. Also, even within an individual, different tissues and organs

                    The Science of Why We Age

age at different rates, so the idea of a single biological age for a person is misleading.

If someone has a serious disease such as cancer, they will be willing to take drugs with quite nasty side effects to avoid dying. Therapeutics for ageing have a much higher bar. We would be asking someone to take a treatment for a very long time on the promise that at the end of ten or twenty years, they may get another ten years of healthy life. This means that the long-term safety of these possible treatments needs to meet a higher standard.

Healthspan, the number of healthy years that we live (as opposed to lifespan, how long we live), is the focus of much anti-ageing research. The idea is called 'compression of morbidity'. The years of poor health are compressed into a very short period at the end of our lives – we live very healthily and then go into a rapid decline and die. However, there is no evidence that compression of morbidity is actually possible. All of the advances in human health in the last decades have left us spending as many or more years in poor health. It is equally possible that advances in combating ageing merely postpone the period of morbidity and possibly even lengthen it.

Even in the best case, if we improve our own health- and lifespan, we need to consider the potential negative consequences for society as a whole. Currently there is considerable economic disparity in longevity in the UK, with the richest 10 per cent of the population living about ten years longer than the poorest 10 per cent. In the United States, which does not have universal health care, it is more like fifteen years. Unless new advances are made equitably available, it could increase disparity even more.

Increased longevity will also raise issues of intergenerational fairness. Already, people accumulate wealth, power and influence as they grow older. In a society where people continue to be healthy and productive over an even longer life, coupled with continued reduction of fertility rates, there will be very slow intergenerational change and transfer of power.

In the long run, with the enormous growth and investment in longevity research, and the increasingly powerful tools of molecular and cell biology, aided perhaps by computational methods including AI, it would be surprising if we do not make real advances in tackling ageing. In my view, interventions that extend healthy years of life are likely to emerge in the foreseeable future,

    The Science of Why We Age

while those that extend lifespan dramatically will prove much more difficult than the optimists assume. Both societally and scientifically, the ageing field is at a threshold, and we need to be prepared both for the benefits that it will bring but also the unintended consequences of success.

Ageing in the Past

by **Molly Conisbee**

My grandmother, Ann Baer, died in December 2021 at the age of 107. It was a great privilege to know someone who remained lively (almost) to the end and was interested and opinionated about the experiences of living a long life. While sometimes frustrated about the physical compromises of ageing (particularly her fading eyesight, as she was someone who loved to draw and sew), she did like to share the long historical perspective that living for over a century had given her. She was mistress of the anecdote and had a mine of stories that brought the feel of her changing century alive. I remember her telling me about a great-uncle who experienced similar longevity, who had been born around 1830 and died in 1930. He was asked shortly before his death what the most important innovation of his lifetime had been. He apparently replied braiding rather than twisting wicks in candles – a new technique from sometime in the mid-nineteenth century, enabling people to work and read after dark without having to regularly pause their activity to trim the candle wick.[1]

It surprised me that he had alighted on this. Living through a period of rapid industrialisation, a world war – surely there were more astonishing things witnessed over the course of such a long life? But, on reflection, and as I have reached my own mid-century during a time of accelerated innovation and technology, I feel rather more in tune with his response. Perhaps it is the quotidian, the everyday, the ordinary – and not tectonic political, social and economic changes – which *really* shapes our daily experiences as we age. And in other ways his answer should not surprise me at all. As well as researching social history, I work as a counsellor, with a particular focus on older age and bereavement. When I listen to clients relate their experiences, what frequently strikes me are the ways in which we reassess our relationship to our own sense of history as we get older. Some clients discover deep wells of empathy and compassion for their parents, or other older people they knew when growing up. When I dive into the archives and am confronted by the challenges our forebears faced in ageing, it can be a humbling and enlightening experience. What I'm learning is that getting older can bring many gifts, including shifts of perspective: a long view that can be both personal and political.

How we age, how it feels to age, and how old age is viewed, has always been intimately bound up with the intersectionality of class, gender, ethnicity, geography, genetics, access to medical care

– a whole host of factors. Due to lack of formal record keeping we don't always have really robust data about longevity in the past, but we do know that by the eighteenth century around 10 per cent of the population (in Europe at least) made it well into their sixties, seventies and beyond.[2] There have always been numerous reasons why individuals might not live very long – accidents, risky working conditions, complications during pregnancy or childbirth, disease, infections, war or famine to name a few – but despite all these life-limiting factors, in previous centuries there were still plenty of people who experienced their 'three score years and ten', as a stroll around any graveyard or cemetery will reveal.

Ageing is a biological fact, but the different phases of life, including old age, are also culturally and historically located concepts, open to interpretation and influenced by factors such as religion, science, economics and society. In that sense our ideas and attitudes towards old age have never been fixed, and ageing has always been approached with a mixture of emotions including veneration, awe, anxiety and even ridicule. The processes of ageing – the slowing of our physical and mental capacities, the greying or loss of hair and the loosening of skin – was, from ancient times until well into the seventeenth century, understood to be caused by imbalances in the four humours of blood, phlegm, yellow bile and black bile. It was believed that as people aged, their body lost heat, so while babies were warm and moist, older people were drier and cooler, due to an abundance of phlegm and black bile (black bile was also associated with melancholy, believed to be a particular affliction of old age). These temporal and physical changes might be somewhat alleviated by alterations to diet and undertaking gentle exercise and regular massages. But they were also to be accepted philosophically as part of the natural cycle of birth and death, decay and renewal. *What's the life of a man, any more than a leaf? A man has his seasons, so why should he grieve?* as a popular, if fatalistic, folk ditty put it.

By the eighteenth century, theories of ageing had moved beyond the idea of imbalanced humours, towards a more recognisably modern 'biological' understanding of the physical changes that we undergo, and their impacts on the body and mind. 'Melancholy' was still associated with old age, another historical link which greatly interests me in my counselling work. The causes of our contemporary age-related melancholy might seem obvious – the failing body and mind – and longevity means that many more of us will face frightening things like cancer or dementia, for example. In older age, we are also more likely to have experienced the deaths of the people we love, we may grieve our loss of professional or familial status, face greater financial precarity, or simply hate the fact that physically everything seems to be 'spreading out or falling out'; *the afternoon knows what the morning never suspected*, as a quotation attributed to poet Robert Frost puts it.[3] But that melancholia was so empathetically *recognised* in the past as an issue for older people, well before the therapeutic approaches of today, is for me a touching bridge of understanding that reaches across the centuries, holding a space for the sadness that can sometimes accompany the passing of years.

As well as growing scientific understanding about the ageing process, social and economic changes during the eighteenth and nineteenth centuries also impacted on cultural perceptions of old age. When old age 'began' remained a relatively fluid concept – regardless of background, life was physically a great deal more arduous in the past, so what we might interpret as some of the signifiers of age today – declining eyesight, arthritis, joint stiffness – were more prevalent for people from a younger age.[4] At the same time, an increasing sense of 'individualism' can be seen in some of the depictions of old age in art and literature. The popularity of the eighteenth-century 'conversation piece', an informal portrait often showing several generations of the same family enjoying domestic pleasures such as taking tea or playing cards, is an example of this. Compared to previous generations, portraiture, while still the preserve of the better-off, had become much more affordable to the rapidly growing merchant and middle classes, and what better way to portray their success than through quietly opulent domestic interiors in which beautiful clothes, porcelain, silverware and furniture (many of these products being the fruits of colonial careers and investments) might be discreetly displayed as though one had casually joined the family for refreshments. Such pieces often portrayed an older couple with their grown-up children and grandchildren, clearly enjoying their material comforts and longevity – in other words, an enlightened, well-upholstered celebration of multi-generational success with age as its centrepiece.

The rise of the idea of age in and of itself as a reflection of success can also be seen through changes to obituary and epitaph. Prior to the eighteenth century, memorial architecture was largely confined to the aristocracy and wealthy, and even then, a burial plaque or headstone might simply state a person's name and date of death. The moment of one's passing was God's will and accepted as such. But by the later eighteenth century, it became fashionable to have a long epitaph describing an individual's professional or academic success, family achievements and notable personal characteristics. To reach great age was celebrated, even more so if an illness towards the end was borne with Christian forbearance. Age was *significant* in a way that it had not quite been to previous generations, because to reach old age was itself a triumph. In the rational, enlightened world, it suggested vigour, health, a worldly status worthy of sharing with future generations.

While ageing might demand some personal resets (there's a charming list of resolutions for old age written by Jonathan Swift at the ripe old age of 34, in which he promises not to marry a much younger woman, talk too much about himself or endlessly repeat his anecdotes, among other things), growing older was also considered a positive advantage, at least for men in professions such as the law, medicine and academia.

Wisdom and insight came with age, even if this fact was not unequivocally accepted (for example, William Hogarth mocked doddery old judges in his 1758 painting *The Bench*). Representations of older women were similarly divided. The contented grandmother, the charitable Christian philanthropist and the sober widow were all celebrated images of female old age. But women were also mocked for trying to look 'younger' than they were with make-up and 'inappropriate' clothes, for becoming 'gigolo-hunting old crones', or bitter spinsters, all recognisable tropes into our own time.[5]

Regardless of century, older age has always carried with it the risk of financial precarity and poverty. Before the introduction of the stringently means-tested Old Age Pension in 1909, and later, in 1948, the welfare state, which introduced the National Health Service (NHS), many older people had to continue to work long after what we might consider a reasonable retirement age today. If frailty or ill health prevented their ability to earn a living, the only recourse might be to request charity from the parish, or worse, to enter the workhouse, which around 20 per cent of the over-sixties were doing by the mid-nineteenth century. The idea of a supportive, loving extended family caring for their elders is something of a sentimental Victorian myth. High child mortality meant that many parents outlived their children. And surviving adult children often moved far away from the parental home to seek work and opportunities to better their lot. A large family was no guarantee of a secure older age.

The workhouse was regarded with particular horror because of its degrading regime and punitive approach towards managing poverty, and it must have felt deeply upsetting and unsettling for those older people who were forced to enter it. After the introduction of the Poor Law Amendment Act of 1834, many of the smaller, old 'poor houses' were amalgamated into larger institutions, some of which housed many hundreds of inmates. Men, women and children were separated from each other, although older couples were sometimes allowed to stay together as there was no danger of procreation. Regardless of age, if they were able to work at all, inmates were expected to earn their keep with repetitive, tedious work, like breaking rocks or unpicking tar-soaked ropes.

Precarity in old age was not just an experience of the economically disadvantaged. During the nineteenth and early twentieth centuries, there were, according to census data, more wom-

     Ageing in the Past

en than men. This resulted in a rather panicky mid-nineteenth century debate about the 'problem' of so-called 'surplus women', and what was to be done about the lack of husbands for them.[6] Unmarried women, unless they were independently wealthy, had to work, and concerns were raised that their employment might create alarming levels of self-sufficiency, financial and otherwise. In fact, single or widowed middle-class women whose families were unwilling or unable to support them had very few financial options. Barred from the physical labour of their working-class sisters, their routes to employment were mainly limited to teaching, either in schools or private homes, or as housekeepers or paid companions. Later, Florence Nightingale's 1860s reforms meant nursing was considered just about respectable enough for unmarried middle-class women.

On reaching retirement, or when they otherwise became perceived to be too old to execute their duties, many women were left with little in savings and no pension. In the 1930s, the campaigner and food writer Florence White would establish the National Spinsters' Pension Association (NSPA), an astonishingly vocal movement which had 104 branches and 140,000 members by 1938 and achieved success in securing pensions for spinsters aged 60, in 1940. But before White's campaign, many women were reliant on institutions like Partis College, established in Bath in 1824 by philanthropist Ann Partis. The college accommodated middle-class women over the age of 50 who were 'reduced and in the decline of life', and admission required applicants to submit testimonials (usually from clergy), baptism certificates and, if applicable, death certificates of fathers or husbands, to demonstrate their suitability for a supported older age. I like to think they found companionship and solidarity in their later years, particularly as some of the entry forms suggest individuals had been more or less abandoned by their families.

Indeed, over many years of researching in archives I have always been fascinated by the ways in which people have adapted to the processes of ageing, finding forms of resilience and support for one another. Domestic arrangements in the eighteenth and nineteenth centuries, for example, often reveal households entirely made up of older people, sometimes related to one another, sometimes former work colleagues, or strangers. These kinds of arrangements spread the financial cost of maintaining a home, but also meant people offered one another company, support and a sense of respectability for the outside world. Given the number of years some folk apparently chose to live together, we can perhaps dare to assume that friendships were also fostered in these environments. Age can in and of itself be a way of forging allyship, as we find safe spaces to reminisce and share what we have experienced and learned along the path of life. And these kinds of communities of the past can perhaps offer us maps for the future as well, in terms of exploring different, communal ways of coping with older age now. We can't necessarily rely on the nuclear family unit any more – because of environmental, social or economic constraints – but it is heartening to think that history might offer us roadmaps of caring.

In our own time, at least in the wealthier countries of the global North, we are living longer and (mostly) healthier lives, although the fruits of longevity are not evenly spread. Life expectancy has tended to diverge between people in wealthier areas, who are living longer, while in economically deprived areas, it declines.[7] How should we be supported in older age, and who should pay for our care? This appears to be a nettle that politicians of all persuasions are unwilling to grasp. Where is the balance of responsibility between us as individuals, and the societal collective in taking care of us as we age? And even for those of us who have extended families, there remain no guarantees that children and grandchildren will live nearby (would we want them to be our 'carers' in any case?). So how do we support the emotional and practical needs of our older communities?

I would suggest, through intertwining some learnings from historical research and therapeutic practice, there are some simple ways in which we might do this. Like the braided candle wick that so improved the night light in the nineteenth century, innovations in our ways of relating and caring for each other need not be so very spectacular. For example, there is a great power in listening to each other, in an active way – something we sometimes forget in the cacophony of contemporary and ever more ubiquitous distracting technology. Active listening is one of the first things we learn to do in counselling training, as a way of really trying to hear and see the person or people in the room with us. How often do we take the time to ask older people what might help them stay fitter, emotionally happier, more able to get out and about? How many spaces do we provide in which different generations can mix, in a place of equality and genuine interaction (composer John Cage suggested combining nursing homes with nurseries, for example). How can we challenge lazy stereotypes about old age, particularly in our increasingly multicultural society, in which different communities bring diverse attitudes towards ageing? What would a society that genuinely valued old age look and feel like?

In many ways the questions that reside with our ageing society of the twenty-first century would seem very familiar to those who came before us. Poverty in older age, how we look after people at different stages of the life cycle, and how we view and represent older age, are as live and politically charged for us today as they were for previous generations and centuries. A society that has grown, at least since the eighteenth century, much more individualistic and therefore, perhaps, ever more *anxious* about the implications of old age (*How did it get so late so soon?* asked Dr. Seuss), needs to find ways and spaces to safely explore what a humane, responsible and equitable 'society of the third age' might look like, both for its older *and* younger inhabitants. Most of us will get to experience old age, and talking about, listening and reflecting on the experiences it can yield are a wonderful foundation for compassionate allyship across the generations.

The Fight to Get Old

by **Travis Alabanza**

'My boobs are sagging,' says an Elder, 'like everyone else around me!'

'*Ha!* I've got lines on my skin I didn't have last week!' another Elder barks, mouth half full of crisps.

'*Lines*? Try *creases*!' heckles a different Elder. 'This body is creasing in ways I didn't think a body could crease.' The laugh that erupts out of her brightens the room, much like the box-dyed purple hair and bright orange cane she's made her uniform.

'Got *another* operation on my eye,' another moans, her voice gravelly from the cigarette hanging out of her mouth. 'At least the doctor is hot!'

'I've gotta get my hip done in a month,' the Elder with the sagging boobs says. Then she tosses her hair back and quips, 'At least when I got my pussy there was something to celebrate after!'

I'm at dinner with a group of older trans women. All of them would scorn me for calling them Elders, but before the dinner has even started, I know it is a title they've earned.

This dinner was supposed to be a roast but no one in the room could cook. The meal feels like an afterthought, and the centrepiece is an ashtray. The house itself is ageing: cracks in the windows and mould on the walls. The room's lighting is struggling, a bulb flickering each time a voice reaches a certain decibel, but I don't think any space with these women could ever feel dull, or stale.

I was invited tonight by a friend of mine, the Elder with sagging boobs. She is 72 years old and medically transitioned at 45. I am 29 while writing this. For the last ten years of my life, I have been out as trans and living as gender non-conforming, and over the course of the last year, I have decided to medically transition. That is, I have started hormone replacement therapy: I am trying to remove the testosterone in my body and replace it with oestrogen. Well, at least make the oestrogen the main girl hanging around.

I am at a table full of people whom I share words with. Words that now in this context mean something. Trans. Transitioning. Cross-dresser. Transvestite. Transgender. Woman. Faggot. Freak. Queer. Deviant. Human. All words that have slid out our own mouths or been hurled at us by others. It bonds us.

But I am also the youngest in the kitchen by at least forty years. The women cackling around this table have been alive double the time that I have been on this Earth. I think of how long my life has already felt. I do not think my life has gone quickly. I can recount endless things that have happened and I cannot believe there is a table of people around me who lived more life than I can comprehend.

Somewhere in between another cigarette being rolled, a roast chicken being abandoned and countless glasses of wine chugged, I pluck up the courage to push my head above the chorus of Elders. My mother always taught me to respect those older than me, so I wait for the gap between dessert and coffee, because who knows how long I have before one of the Elders will involuntarily fall asleep. Age does that, you know.

'How did you do it?' I squeak. Something about my age in this context makes me nervous.

'Do what? Gotta be more specific than that, baby,' quips the Elder with the purple box dye hair. The pet name here feels like it's doing its job.

'Keep going. Like, keep changing,' I reply.

Trust the most terminally online person at the table to kill the mood. Normally I'd be in favour of telling a joke or some salacious gossip about a Z-list celebrity I met in the dark room of a London club, but I know how rare it is to be surrounded by this much wisdom so casually and I don't want to waste it. Or, to be more honest, I

   The Fight to Get Old

don't want to waste the chance for their powers to rub off on me. I see all the Elders laughing freely. Dexterous in their ability to jump from the dark shadows of their past to the brightness of their present lives. I observe them speak of the death of friends, loss of limbs, precarity of future, longing for the past – all while ensuring they have faces worn by laughter.

'Like, push through the noise,' I add.

On the bus journey to dinner, I did the usual regrettable action of scrolling on my phone instead of reading. I was met with a cacophony of assaults. A petition is doing the rounds about whether or not trans people should be allowed to use the mixed pond at Hampstead Heath. A newspaper article is talking about the pressure gender clinics are under and how the wait time to see a gender specialist in some cities is recorded to be over seventy years. A GoFundMe is being circulated to pay for my friend's top surgery, while another is circulating to raise money for a performer who was attacked on their way home. The assassination of a prominent far-right political figure has people trying desperately to pin it on the transgender community. The cost of my private hormones that I thought I was privileged enough to obtain have doubled. I am not sure what I will do.

I know I am not the only person scrolling on their phone wondering, *where do we go from here? How can we continue?* Transphobia is not the only thing rising on the planet: heat and water levels. Man-made disasters they will call natural. Genocides denied in plain sight. A growing divide in our society that sometimes feels too wide to try and tape up.

But as I observe the Elders around the table all night, I feel ashamed for wanting to give up. I project onto their history a struggle that I am sure I can only mythologise in writing rather than actually imagining. I hear of the friends they lost to AIDS, the backstreets they had to inject themselves in with hormones to *change*, the jobs they had to lose, the attackers they had to run from, the lives they had to hide – and I want to gag the internal voice of mine that wants to give up. I instead want to know how they do it, how they keep going.

One of the Elders lights up a cigarette and lets out a deep exhalation of smoke. A sigh clouding the room.

'What other choice do we have?' she says to me, with both softness and surety. 'We keep going.'

'But what if they stop us? What if—'

　　　　　　　　　　The Fight to Get Old

I'm interrupted by another Elder: 'Fuck, if they tried! You can't stop what's natural. Sure, you can make it harder. Sure, you can make it fucking hell. But it doesn't stop us. We find another way.'

I am about to ask another question but one of the Elders starts talking about a book she has been reading. She raises the first word of her sentence loud enough to let me know the conversation is moving on. It isn't rude, or dismissive, it is an understanding of how to keep the light bulbs glimmering, rather than dimming around the table. A little wink at me, as if the Elder is saying, 'Let us keep living, not dwelling.'

So I let them live. As I watch them jump again from topic to topic, repeating a story they already told at the beginning of the night, forgetting the names of friends and frequently using outdated words that on a good day are a bit questionable, and on a bad day, outright offensive. I nod, and try not to dwell on the task I felt burdened with. That is, the task of ageing as a trans person. The task of survival. In order to age, I will have to first survive. I try not to dwell on which governments are eradicating our rights, or sink too hard into the hole in my pockets caused by the increase in the price of our hormones, or spiral too deep into my screen of debates about where we should and shouldn't be allowed. I try to live in the moment in front of me. The Elders with sagging chests, and creasing lines, and bellies that have dropped as evidence that they have eaten. I try to live by their proof that we have always found a way to keep going, like a stream determined to find its way to the ocean. How natural it is, despite all the different ways to get there.

Hours have passed and most of the Elders have either gone home or are napping on sofas in the living room, stopping to sleep midway through a conversation. I think about how I cannot wait to get to an age where I can sleep wherever I want without an excuse. How the elderly have earned the right to nap wherever they want.

The Elder with the orange cane comes to pour me one last glass of wine. She has clearly learned the lesson of savouring every last drop in a bottle.

'We haven't got a choice, but to keep going,' she says. 'I knew I had to transition when I realised I couldn't imagine myself ageing. Like, people at school would talk about growing old, and getting jobs, and becoming parents, and having futures – and until I transitioned, I couldn't imagine any of it. Until I became who I knew I was, there wasn't any future.'

I look up ready to reply, but she is already hobbling out of the room. My grandmother used to do that too. Leave and enter rooms without announcing herself. Maybe something about ageing means you no longer have time for the things that do not matter.

I am left alone at the table. The fragments of conversations simmer somewhere with the discarded chicken. I am sad to see the Elders go, yet I know that their departure is part of the cycle. In order to enjoy the presence of those older than us we have to also accept the sadness of when they leave.

I can feel their presence still with me, lingering in the cloud of smoke – Elders always have a habit of leaving a trace.

It is natural. Like their boobs sagging. Their bodies become harder to operate. Eyesight worsening. Words going out of date. It all feels natural. Yet despite ageing being the most natural occurrence, it's not a given for everyone. Some people have to fight for it.

There is so much chatter about where to put the elderly. The front of the bus. Or in a house away from our homes. Governments worried about the economics of an ageing population. Yet when I look at these women around me at dinner, I remember some people have to push past governments, and legislation, and doctors, and sceptics, and isolation, and ostracisation, and exile, and psychiatrists, and violence and a raft of other things to still be here. They have to carve out a place for themselves to age, and then work so hard to make it happen. They have to use the magic of imagining themselves into the future. How brave these women have been to see something out of the unseen. While being told it is impossible to live, they have dared to keep living this long. They do it all, while still knowing how to host a dinner party full of belly laughs.

My mother always taught me to write a note to thank an Elder for having you at their house for dinner. It is the sign of a good guest.

I leave a note on the table, unsure of when I will see the women again. The note says, simply:

We will keep living, not dwelling.

Yours, Someone who hopes to age and will fight like hell to do it.

Ageing and Care

by **Lynne Segal**

Can we ever celebrate ageing? It's a question I have long pondered, given that we know that in the wider world almost everyone is worrying about growing old, and at ever younger ages. Moreover, apparently what frightens people most – more than their fear of dying – is the notion of increased dependency. That leads me at once to another question I have often addressed: can we seriously value caring? We know that caring overall, especially hands-on caring, has always been undervalued, traditionally seen as the role of women or 'servants', with those able to often choosing to avoid caring work. Now both questions *could* be answered positively, were we to appreciate the value of a long life, along with the fact that varying forms of dependency are a feature of our lives from the beginning. However, there is so much still to do in getting us there, on a journey that recognises that both ageing and caring are inherently political, but will only be valued in a world that is almost the inverse of the one we now occupy. It is in that alternative realm that it is possible to imagine ageing radically while appreciating that caring is one of the most basic and significant of all human actions, often challenging but usually rewarding. Let me try to take you there, surveying the many hazards along the way.

The most obvious problem is the enduring prevalence of the notion of ageing as inevitable decline. Now as we'll see, this view of ageing has been contested by many, especially over recent decades, suggesting rather that old age could, and should, be seen as offering possibilities for better judgement and greater freedom or satisfaction. However, any overall possibility for a pleasant and comfortable old age can be undermined nowadays due to decades of declining welfare support, which impact most heavily on the lives of more vulnerable people. In this time of deep inequality there is a huge discrepancy in healthy life expectancy between the rich and the poor, with the wealthiest people in the UK experiencing up to nineteen more years of good health compared to those in the most deprived areas, according to data analysis by the British charity the Health Foundation. Thus, while advances in medical science have granted many of us longer and healthier lives in old age, this outcome exists today alongside the ill health and distressing poverty faced by less affluent or stigmatised groups. Public calls for people to remain fit, healthy and apparently youthful, by any means possible, merely sideline this distressing reality. They accompany official encouragement for the elderly to volunteer in charitable causes, and to shoulder more childcare duties if they have grandchildren. But any emphasis on elderly well-being, by whatever means, is subverted by the existence of comprehensive and widespread ageism. Research tells us that negative attitudes towards and discrimination against the elderly have increased along with growing longevity. Thus, instead of social celebration of our possible longer lives, including exceptional longevity becoming increasingly common in some of the richer countries (as in Canada, for example, where those who reach 100 are the fastest-growing age group), we face the existence of increased ageism. Indeed, in recent years the Royal Society for Public Health described ageism as 'the most commonly experienced form of prejudice and discrimination in the UK'.

It was an American psychiatrist and gerontologist, Robert N. Butler, who first coined the term ageism back in 1969, referring to both individual attitudes that perpetuate harmful images of the elderly and institutional practices that discriminate against them. The following year, Simone de Beauvoir published her book *Old Age* (*La Vieillesse*). Such was the dread those two words provoked that when translated into English two years later publishers changed its title to *The Coming of Age*. Yet over the last half-century there have been frequent attempts, including my own in my 2013 book *Out of Time: The Pleasures and Perils of Ageing*, to oppose this prejudice – so far, producing little, or no, change. It's a sad and perplexing situation when we will all grow old, short of an early death, hence ageism will soon enough become prejudice against ourselves. Yet all the latest reports on ageing still find hostile associations with older people dominate every area of society, including the media, advertising, and central and local government. Indeed, they are present across every age group, including the elderly, although strongest of all in middle age. Thus, the closer we come to that fluctuating defi-nition, the definitively 'old', the greater the aver-sion people express towards the 'elderly'.

This is surely why the very first thing old people often say when interviewed about their experiences of ageing is simply, 'I don't feel old' – whatever their age. Such are the pejorative con-notations clustering around old age that the char-ity director of Age UK today, when interviewed a few years ago, said she never uses the word 'old', while adding that it is only alright to speak of be-ing 'older'. This seems extremely disconcerting from a charity dedicated to promoting positive images of old age. The rapid growth in repulsion towards the use of the term 'old' is also why Age Concern renamed itself in 1971, discarding its original name – the Old People's Welfare Committee – from when it was first set up, with high hopes, by the independent feminist MP Eleanor Rathbone in 1940. Thus, our first main struggle remains trying to combat ageism. We also need to understand its underlying gendered dynamics, both because women are seen, wrongly, as the more fragile sex and because women are associated with the work of care.

It's always useful to know the history behind any form of prejudice. One historian who has written widely on ageism is Pat Thane, who is also an authority on the development of the British welfare state and the adequacy and shortcomings of its support for the elderly. Thane notes that while elderly people have consistently faced discrimination over the last century, its impact varies by gender, class and ethnicity. Women especially have been subjected to earlier retirement and age-related bias, sometimes as early as their thirties, although similar signs of early ageing were ignored in men in the workplace. Today, we do find more older women in the workforce, though their position is often somewhat precarious, and they will be the first to lose their jobs if savings are required. Moreover, it is still the case today, as it was in the past, that more women than men can be found living in poverty in old age, a situation that has not changed greatly over the last century. Thane notes that, since their inception in 1909, UK state pensions have never been sufficient to live on, and that women overall have tended to receive lower work pensions than men, usually having received lower pay in their jobs while their caring commitments routinely interrupted their working lives. Perhaps unsurprisingly, therefore, with the recent cuts in welfare since 2010, longevity has begun falling for the poorest 20 per cent of the population, predominantly old women living in poverty.

An additional pitfall of living in poverty, although not reducible simply to poverty, is the likelihood of old women's greater loneliness. We know that it is older women who are the most likely to end up living alone, which is especially hard for those with financial constraints. Government data in recent years reveals that in the UK 60 per cent of women over 75 live alone, compared to 13 per cent of the whole population,[8] and that those who do live alone are more likely to feel lonely, including the half a million older women today who say they are severely lonely. This was exacerbated not only by Covid in recent years, but also by the ongoing cutback of welfare and local government provision, which has meant the closing down of many of the community resources where older people might once have gathered, whether in lunch clubs or day-care centres.

Yet there have also been many attempts to combat ageism and improve living conditions for the elderly, which of course means working on many fronts. First up we need to hear many more stories of the differing experiences of ageing, which of course is not always easy given that many of us prefer not to think about it and that older people, especially women, are often rendered invisible. Moreover, despite the stereotypical assumptions of physical and mental weakness, along with increasing 'ugliness', underpinning the legendary derision projected onto 'old ladies', the reality is we all age differently, becoming even less alike in old age. Thus, today we can find many more stories from people calling themselves 'ageist resisters', those determined to tackle our continuing amplified cultural aversion towards even discussing old age. They are overwhelmingly old women who, as we know, remain the prime targets of gerontophobia. I am thinking of some of my recently departed heroines, such as Ursula Le Guin, who was also determined to celebrate old age: 'For old people, beauty doesn't come free with the hormones, the way it does for the young ... It has to do with who the person is. More and more clearly it has to do with what shines through those gnarly faces and bodies.'[9] As Le Guin knows, it is not any loss of beauty, always such a culturally inflected term, but the loss of identity and belonging that old people must fight to transcend, while also attempting to preserve former ways of engaging with the world or finding new ways of relating.

We surely know that any radical narratives of ageing must begin with rejecting today's continuing market mindset suggesting that after retiring from waged work we become 'unproductive', and hence less valuable in the world. On the contrary, old people have often found many ways of living well, when they have the resources to do so, and when those in need of care can have their needs met. Another flamboyant ageist resister is the Jewish lesbian activist Joan Nestle (born in the US but now living in Melbourne, Australia), praiseworthy for her determined celebration of desire in old age, something many older women often find hard to mention, let alone applaud. In her book *A Fragile Union*, written over twenty-five years ago when she was first ill with cancer, Nestle still determinedly presented a desiring self to the world, even as she recorded her own bodily weaknesses and her dependency on others for care. Thus, in her late fifties, and starting a new relationship, Nestle writes: 'Grey hair and textured hands are now erotic emblems I seek out ... I find this to be a time of great passion in my life, a time of increased commitments to the forging of fragile solidarities.'

However, as all ageist resisters know, we must tread carefully when meditating on possibilities for expressing desire, pleasure and living well in old age, given the vast disparities in possibilities for different groups of women. It can be especially perplexing amid the deluge of market promises pretending we can stay 'forever young', buying products from the massively profitable longevity industry. No one was more critical of these invasive, class- and race-blind 'rejuvenating' regimes than the now much-missed feminist Barbara Ehrenreich. Approaching 80, in her last book, *Natural Causes* (2018), she ridiculed the widely promoted fiction that we can stay in full control of our minds and bodies with a little more self-love and self-care. What Ehrenreich insisted upon, when she was interviewed in her late seventies, was that *mutual* care, not *self*-care, is what we need if we are to live a good life at any age: 'We could talk to each other, we could have more parties and celebrations, we could do more dancing. I know this sounds a little crazy, but I think that it's something that's very much missing in our lives.'

Certainly, to continue to pursue our desires in old age, whatever their nature, takes us to issues of care. Sadly, given the realities of ageism, it is often the elderly whose needs for care are most neglected. Care work, whether paid or unpaid and in whatever setting, remains undervalued, leading to a persistent care crisis today. Many people find themselves in jobs where there is little time to care adequately, if at all, for family or friends, however much they want to. It is this crisis of care that formed the basis for the popular and widely translated manifesto I helped to write, *The Care Manifesto* (2020). It is a call to arms, suggesting the need to place issues of care at the very heart of our politics and economy. Here – like other feminists before us – we again questioned the notion of 'productivity', insisting that caring, defined in the broadest terms, is not only productive in its maintenance of life, but is also a way of relating to others and to non-human life that enriches all our personal interactions across the lifespan, as well as working towards a sustainable world.

Thankfully, today, such thoughts are heard more often. A few years ago, the US ageing activist Ashton Applewhite published her joyful celebration, *This Chair Rocks: A Manifesto Against Ageism*. It calls for us all to celebrate old age, and to join her in exposing ageist myths knowing that the sooner growing older is stripped of reflexive dread, the easier it will be for us to appreciate the countless ways in which we can enjoy old age, enriching us all. We always need to keep expanding our imaginations on the multiple ways of confronting old age, always knowing that whatever our age we need to try to savour each moment as it passes, while also trying to embrace life with all the love, friendship, openness and care for each other that we can muster. Indeed, battling the stigma of ageing is itself one way to keep passion alive in old age, however we identify. Political resistance is also a way of keeping us alive to life itself, whatever our age, health or fragility. We saw this first expressed over half a century ago in the deliberate provocations of Maggie Kuhn, who founded the Gray Panthers movement in the US in 1970, in order to flout the frequent dismissal of the post-menopausal woman. But then this life-long union activist, sex radical, peace campaigner and civil rights advocate was determined, as she said towards the end of her long life, to do something outrageous every day. Her provocations included not just insisting upon the frequently renounced reality of older women's sexuality but also continuing to engage in all the old battles she had fought throughout her long life.

With the World Health Organization recently calling for the development of a global campaign to combat ageism and outlining the need for all states to build cities that would be as accessible and welcoming for old people as they are for young people, we know we have much to keep us busy, whatever our age.

Who Gets to Age Well?

by **Pragya Agarwal**

We will all age. This is the inevitable truth. Our cells age: we encounter degradation of telomeres that results in degradation of our biological and physiological functions. But so many of us fear it. The 'ageing anxiety'[10] is quite distinct from the fear of death. This anxiety is the fear of the loss of our mental, physical and cognitive functions as we age. It is also associated, particularly in women, with worries around the loss of good looks, of wrinkles and sagging skin, of losing worth in society that attributes so much capital to a youthful appearance. We are bombarded with ads for anti-ageing beauty products, the idea being that somehow we should try our very best to reverse the natural ageing process, or at least be able to pause it, like Dorian Gray. Ageism affects us all.

There are multimillionaires, like Bryan Johnson, for instance, who are trying to reverse ageing. His 'Project Blueprint' is a longevity programme with a strict regime of diet and exercise, combined with technology, aiming to reverse the chronological age of his body and attain the biological age of 18 again. He is currently 48 years old. He is spending almost 2 million dollars per year on doing this, with the support of more than thirty highly qualified scientists at his disposal every day. Most people cannot afford this. Johnson has the luxury to manage ageing. But is this really 'ageing well'? Healthy ageing isn't merely living longer, but living a happy life with minimal emotional, mental or physical setbacks. The number of years we live versus a good quality of life. I know what I would choose. Yes, such a strict lifestyle can be bought with money, but there is no evidence that Johnson has a good quality of life, and there is no guarantee that his genetics would not play a role in the way he ages. We still don't know enough about this to be able to manage the ageing process. But everyone, irrespective of their means, should be able to age in the best way possible and live a happy, healthy life for as long as they live. Instead, most people live with the fear of ageing as they grow older, with this anxiety peaking as people begin to reach their forties.

One of the main reasons for this rising anxiety is the ageism in our society. In Western pre-nineteenth-century society, older people, both men and women, were generally held in high esteem and considered to be authoritative and with a life experience of value to others. But with industrialisation, where speed and efficiency became connected to capital, older people were suddenly considered to be of less value, and we see a downward shift in the way older people are perceived and treated in society since the early 1900s.

Ageism is rife in our society, ubiquitous and insidious, because it largely goes unnoticed or unchallenged. A 2021 World Health Organization report showed that every second person in the world holds at least some ageist beliefs. Analysis of more than 1 billion words from media databases across the US and the UK showed that there were six times as many negative descriptions as positive ones, the main ten descriptors of older adults being: *frail, infirm, housebound, dementing, long-stay, disabled, spinster, aging, childless, vulnerable.*[11]

At the same time, our society is growing older, as we are living longer. Between now and 2050, the number of people over 60 is expected to double, while the number of individuals aged 80 or older is projected to triple. In the UK the median age rose from 33.9 years in 1974 to 40.7 years by 2022, and one in five people today are over 65.[12] The United Nations has marked this decade (2021–30) as the decade of healthy ageing. The goal is for older people to be valued and to live with dignity and confidence wherever they might be. While we might think that having more

                              Who Gets to Age Well?

older people might reduce ageism in society, that is not the case.

The Covid-19 pandemic heightened societal ageism and associated self-inflicted anxieties, where much of the public discourse was that it was an 'old person's problem'.[13] Media and political messaging demonised older adults and considered them dispensable. On the one hand, in many countries such as France, the deaths of older people remained undocumented and unreported, as the public health authorities systematically failed to report deaths of residents from nursing homes and care facilities, implying that their deaths were insignificant.[14] And, on the other hand, all older adults were perceived to be equally vulnerable with the public discourse and communication taking a patronising attitudes towards them, reinforcing the ageist views of society. Stricter conditions were imposed on them, which while necessary at times, exacerbated their social isolation and loneliness – as in the Netherlands where special early shopping hours for older people led to legislation proposals to 'isolate the elderly'. Such messages intended to protect elderly people in fact reinforced negative age-related stereotypes where older people were perceived to be frail, carrying a number of morbidities, and therefore of less value with the governmental push on productivity and return to work. The discussion deepened the intergenerational chasm meaning many younger people were resentful of older people for taking up resources, and of the strict lockdown guidelines that restricted their own freedom. A survey across 3,000 adults aged between 35 and 75 years in the UK, carried out in 2022, revealed that more than 60 per cent expressed a deep fear of ageing.[15] While there is sparse data on how it compares to pre-pandemic days, surveys done in 2017 and then again in 2020 with 660 adults between 18 and 30 years old shows that the communication during the pandemic definitely contributed to amplifying and exacerbating negative feelings and anxieties associated with ageing amongst young people. While in 2017, around 12 per cent of the respondents looked forward to ageing, this was only about 2 per cent post-pandemic.[16]

The fear of growing older, that I believe to be a form of internalised, self-directed ageism – has an impact on well-being. The microaggressions associated with being treated unfairly, or being seen as helpless, frail or even unproductive and therefore a burden on society, have a hugely negative influence. The above-mentioned

World Health Organization report showed that older individuals who were exposed to negative age-related stereotypes showed a heightened cardiovascular response to stress. This is possibly due to stereotype embodiment, where members of stigmatised groups internalise and assimilate societal stereotypes about themselves which leads to a degradation of their mental health. Ageism has been linked, globally, to about 6.33 million cases of depression, and cognitive impairment, where people underperform on a task due to worries about confirming a negative stereotype about their group. Older people who feel a stereotype threat are more likely to fail a cognitive test for dementia.[17] While the internalisation of these negative stereotypes can have a huge impact on mental health, it also has consequences for physical and cognitive health. Some 422 studies that collated twenty-five years' worth of data from more than 7 million participants revealed that ageism was associated with poorer health outcomes in 95.5 per cent of the studies. There is also less likelihood of participants engaging with health care actively and seeking treatment in a professional setting if they become ill. The most extreme form of such fear of ageing – gerascophobia – can lead to body dysmorphia due to the fear of loss of physical attractiveness, and an acute feeling of rejection and low self-confidence,[18] resulting in self-imposed social isolation and loneliness.

While ageism is a global issue, it is dependent on geography, gender, race, class and all the intersections that can amplify such marginalisation, in turn impacting who has the privilege to age well, in a healthy supportive manner, and who does not. Even though older people are seen as a homogenous group, they are not. In individualistic societies, for instance, older people are not as revered or cared for as in some collectivist cultures, where there are more close-knit family structures.

There are gender disparities in how old age affects us. Older women are valued much less than older men and encounter more ageism. Age in men is mostly associated with wisdom and gravitas – the 'silver fox' – whereas older women are judged for their wrinkles, their saggy skin, their changing bodies and their clothes, and we hear phrases such as 'mutton dressed as lamb'. Even AI, which of course is a reflection of our society, has shown bias against older women in hiring and recruitment. Women are often in unpaid caregiving roles, working part time or

   Who Gets to Age Well?

taking career breaks for caregiving and parenting responsibilities, and so they often do not accrue as much capital or pension as men of a similar age. Therefore, more of their lives are spent in economic deprivation, especially if they do not have a support system as they grow older. Although women in general live longer than men in most countries around the world,[19] they live with more frailties, chronic pain and ill health. At 65 women can expect to live more than half of their remaining years in poor health, and as they get older this proportion increases.[20] This is more common in cases of women from disadvantaged areas and from minoritised ethnic communities.

Research carried out in Argentina, Colombia, Ethiopia, Lebanon, Malawi, Mozambique, the Philippines, Sri Lanka, Tanzania and Yemen[21] showed that conflict and climate change, along with inflation, are making older people more vulnerable globally. Prices of medicines have gone up between 35 and 70 per cent. Across gender and social lines of inequality, older women are facing greater shortages of food and resources, especially as most women are in unpaid caregiving and domestic roles and therefore do not have any social protection such as pensions.[22] In Ethiopia, for instance, only about 7 per cent of older people receive a pension, of whom only 10 per cent are women. Shortage of medicines and vaccines due to conflict and rising tariffs affect older people most.

Besides the institutional and interpersonal ageism, individual and directed ageism within the health care sector impacts people's physical health. While men suffer from cancer and heart disease more than women, women have higher rates of chronic conditions such as arthritis, depression, osteoporosis and related fractures. Moreover, it takes as much as four years longer for women to be diagnosed with some life-threatening illnesses than men, because pain in women is underestimated. With many of the conditions that are specific to women, such as endometriosis and menopause, still severely under-researched, along with the disadvantages and inequalities they face in life as a result of having lower socioeconomic status than men, women are more anxious, more stressed and can have lower self-esteem as they grow older.[23] According to a Nuffield Trust study, between 2011 and 2025 the gynaecology specialty waiting list in the UK grew by 275 per cent, leaving thousands of women waiting for essential procedures and delayed diagnosis, doomed to years of pain.

    Who Gets to Age Well?

At the start of 2025, more than 580,010 women were waiting over eighteen weeks for their first consultant appointment.[24] Older women can be perceived as frail and helpless, infantilised by medical professionals with no sense of autonomy, and have more aggressive – and effective – treatments withheld from them.[25] It is no surprise that more than half of women over the age of 50 are concerned about accessing medical support because their experiences have been so disappointing. Women carry more 'disease burden', which is increasing as waiting times rise further due to funding cuts to the NHS. As a result, the 'disability-adjusted-life-years' (DALY), a measure of healthy life, as opposed to merely a long life, is much lower in women.

Geography also plays a role. People in the most affluent areas in the UK, both men and women, can live up to eighteen years longer in good health than their counterparts in the most deprived parts of the UK.[26] While there is a demographic divergence in the way the UK is ageing, with more older populations in rural and coastal areas as compared to large cities, those living in rural or coastal areas face more loneliness and have fewer resources and less access to health care. The healthy life expectancy varies between different regions too. The map shows a distinct north/south divide. Men and women living in Scotland, the North of England, East Midlands and Wales tend to have a lower-than-average healthy life expectancy at birth. People living in the South of England and London tend to have a higher-than-average healthy life expectancy at birth, with the difference between the highest and lowest health life expectancy local authority areas as much as 22 years.[27] The North-East has the lowest healthy life expectancy for both men and women.[28]

The aspiration to have a happy healthy older life is rooted in financial security. The increasing cost of living has made these disparities even more acute. A Crisis report from 2025 showed that housing costs were causing havoc with older adults, especially those in retirement age, with many not able to retire because they have no housing security, and more than half of 1,600 surveyed adults from the lower 50th percentile of incomes over the age of 55 were anxious about losing their homes and being in debt to keep the roof over their heads.[29] Older people facing homelessness has risen by over 50 per cent over the past five years.

To make way for housing costs, people

have been cutting down on hobbies and social activities, and even external care and support. This is putting more strain on them mentally and physically but also increasing social isolation and disconnectedness. Age UK research in 2025 showed that more than 90 per cent of older people in the survey were worried about rising costs, and that many had started eating less, or were cutting down on medications and specialist support. More than 80 per cent could not afford to have heating on for long in their houses. This has a multi-fold impact.[30]

As people age and lose muscle mass, especially beyond the age of 65, they need more fat reserves. Extra padding can protect people from fractures as their bones can become weaker and more brittle. And when other illnesses strike, these can be useful energy reserves. Patricia Hewitt, the former UK health secretary, told me at a recent talk that being underweight is more dangerous for people over 65, especially for women, than being obese, as measured by the standard Body Mass Index (BMI) scale, a metric with roots in imperialistic ideas of an ideal body shape and size.[31] The BMI measure can underestimate the height of older people due to spinal curvature and does not distinguish between fat and muscle mass. A BMI that can be considered healthy in a younger person would be dangerous for an older person with their higher risk of mortality. The ageing process and accompanying loss of muscle mass also means that older bodies become less capable of absorbing nutrition and need more warmth for normal physiological functions.

So, when older people cannot afford to eat, and they cannot warm their houses, they are at a much higher risk of malnutrition, and at a risk of dying. The way our cities and neighbourhoods are being designed is contributing to this. Corner shops are dying out, and our road networks are not designed for walking. When older people do not have a support system, do not have shops in easy walking distance, and are unable to access the supermarkets themselves, they can also face starvation. Almost 1.3 million people in the UK above the age of 65, about one in ten, are malnourished or at risk.

Ethnicity also compounds the effects of ageing and ageism. The 2021 census recorded 2.17 million people aged 50 or over with Black, Asian and Minority Ethnic (BAME) backgrounds living in England – an increase of 80 per cent from 2011. And some older people from certain minoritised backgrounds, such as Pakistani and

Bangladeshi, are living with poorer health and in inadequate living conditions as compared to the national average. Working-age adults from minoritised ethnic groups earn less on average than their white counterparts. There is a strong association between poverty and health. There is also shame and guilt associated with poverty that is amplified in certain cultures. Other factors such as racial discrimination with health care settings, lack of language to advocate for themselves, and poorer knowledge and access to health care, as well as a reluctance to self-report health issues due to fear of prejudice and racism, are the primary causes. Racism and racial discrimination not only affect their ability to progress and be secure socially and economically, it also prevents them from seeking help when they need it. They are ageing faster, on par with their white counterparts who are twenty years older.[32]

In a society that is stratified into hierarchies and structured by forms of oppression and an imbalance in power, it is the older people who are some of the worst impacted. Older people are seen to be an economic burden, symbolic of a shrinking workforce. Again, this is very much culture-dependent but in a capitalist society that emphasises productivity as a person's worth and value older people are seen to be less efficient and slower in mental, physical and cognitive capacities. On one hand, they are pushed out of the workforce because of institutional ageism, and on the other hand they are perceived to be an economic burden on state and society. Such ageist attitudes and stereotypes determine who is given adequate care and who is ignored. Broadly, sexism, ageism, racism and other forms of bias intersect to create disrespectful environments for older adults in medicine and health care. Being ill is seen as a natural part of getting older and so care and treatment can be withheld from older people. Most clinical trials have an age cap, so older people are excluded from trials even for diseases that directly impact them, such as cancer, cardiovascular disease and type 2 diabetes.

We all will age. But only a few will have the opportunity to age well, depending on who they are and where they are. While genetics matter and are responsible for about 20 per cent of differences in health in old age, there are other external factors that intertwine and have the most impact on our ability to live longer and healthier. Our lifestyle, which is determined by access to social capital and cohesion, economic resources, education, food, clean air and opportunities

Who Gets to Age Well?

to access health care without fear of discrimination, has the most sway. Individual identities and proximity to power and privilege in terms of class, ethnicity and gender all affect how people age, and how well they can manage the ageing process. As the number of people aged 60 or over worldwide is expected to increase to 1.4 billion in the next five years,[33] if we don't tackle the multiple inequalities, these disparities will widen. It is not enough to have vague goals around ageing well that treat older adults as a homogenous group. We need to tackle ageism and consider the intersectional effects of ageing. Only then will we all age well.

Rethinking Ageing for the Twenty-First Century

by **Andrew J. Scott**

I was born in 1965, when more Britons died before their first birthday than at any other age. Today, the most common age at death is 90. This dramatic change isn't only due to improvements in infant mortality. Over the past sixty years, the chances of a 50-year-old living to 80 have almost doubled. It all adds up to one of the great accomplishments of the modern era: however old you are today, you are likely to live longer than members of any preceding generation.

For most of history, only a minority of any population lived long enough to reach old age. In Britain today, that minority has become a majority. The UK's Office for National Statistics estimates that a baby girl born today has a life expectancy of 90 and a one-in-five chance of reaching 100. Yet this extraordinary gift of lengthening human lives does not come without challenges. The policies and institutions that served previous generations are now facing very different population models. When only a few individuals lived long enough to become very old, there was no real pressure to transform society to accommodate them. However, with many people now likely to live into their ninth, tenth and even eleventh decade, a comprehensive rethink is unavoidable.

The challenge extends far beyond addressing the increasingly unsustainable costs of pensions and health care. Most of all it demands that we consider exactly what we would like to do with the extra years we now have and how to prepare for them. To the long list of decisions that we and our families already make over the life course – when to leave education, whether and when to get married, whether to have children, how to finance housing and what work to do – must be added an issue that, like most of the others, is best not left until too late. How can we make the most of our twenty-first-century longevity?

We can begin by viewing ageing as a blessing, not a curse. In 1900, global life expectancy was 32 years. Today it is over 73. What does this mean in practice? It means we mourn the loss of fewer infants, we see fewer parents die in midlife, and we see more grandparents enjoying their grandchildren. These are the happiest of benefits, albeit accompanied by more complicated trends.

While life expectancy is increasing, birth rates are falling across the world. As a result, the proportions of young and old are shifting, giving rise to concerns about an 'ageing society'. In 1965, approximately one in eight of the UK population was aged 65 or older; only one in fifty was aged 80 or older. Today, those proportions are one in five and one in twenty. By 2065, according to the United Nations, the proportion of older persons will have grown to one in four (for those aged 65+) and one in ten (for those aged 80+).

This demographic reversal is rarely viewed in a positive light. In part, this is due to the common association of ageing with physical decline. In broad terms, the average proportion of life that is healthy has remained roughly constant. While that means more years spent in good health, it also means more years on average at the end of life in poor health. Fears of disease and dementia dampen our enthusiasm for longevity.

The development of an 'ageing society' also stokes concern at the government level of encroaching economic ruin. The establishment of a UK state pension and the introduction of mass retirement were widely seen as major achievements of the twentieth century. But that was then. Today, pension funds are stretching to breaking point. The costs of health care are spiralling. The NHS is tottering. Can we really afford to get much older?

The alarm is understandable, but it tends to overlook the people at the root of the problem. People, for example, like me. In the year I was born, a 60-year-old man had a 40 per cent chance of making it to 80. Today, my chances are closer to 70 per cent. Personally, I'm grateful for an 'ageing society' and I think many others might be, too. As an old Irish proverb puts it: 'Do not resent getting old, many are denied the privilege.'

So how should we deal with the conflicting pleasures and perils of longevity? Should we opt for one last blow-out on fast cars and slow cruise ships, then accept whatever lot our bodies throw at us? Should we continue working as long as possible? Is Mick Jagger, still rocking and rolling at 82, our best octogenarian model?

Given how pervasive the negative view of ageing has become, it's striking how little we focus on improving the way we age. If older people living longer creates problems for all age groups, why isn't there more discussion of radical change, more planning for the later years we can now expect to reach with greater certainty?

Planning by talking about care home expansion, fall alert devices and adult diaper supplies certainly matters, but what is really needed is a broader debate about ways of remaining healthy, active and engaged for longer. Few things are as important for our later years as planning how to enjoy them. If we fear ill health and financial struggles, then why not invest in our future to ensure we can avoid these outcomes?

Tackling this longevity agenda requires multiple changes. First, we need to address this outdated passivity about ageing. We must acknowledge that we can change how we age. One widespread assumption is that becoming old is an event, rather than a process. A long-standing bureaucratic convention picked 65 as the age at which oldness begins, regardless of how young you may feel or behave. This links with a second assumption – that birthdays are the best measure of age. Chronologically, everyone adds a year every 365 days, and we all know exactly how old we are.

However, focusing on chronological age misleads us into thinking that how we age is fixed, whereas in reality, there is considerable variation in the ways people age. One simple example: an individual living in one of the most affluent parts of the UK can expect to live nine years longer than residents of the least affluent areas. The gap is even wider for years spent in good health: wealthier areas offer an eighteen-year advantage over their poorest neighbours. Few statistics are as telling in emphasising that how we age isn't fixed and that we can influence how we age.

Nor is income the only measure that

makes a difference. A host of behavioural, environmental and genetic factors are all part of the longevity equation, resulting in an older generation that is highly diverse. In England, the healthiest 90-year-olds suffer less than half the frailties of the most fragile 50-year-olds. Similarly, the healthiest 70-year-olds are in better shape than the average 50-year-old. Empirical studies suggest that around 80 per cent of how we age is driven by behaviour and the environment; only 20 per cent is genetic. If we fear ageing, then in response to that statistic, we should start to think seriously about what we can do now to ensure we age well.

What does this mean in practice? We cannot control our genes, but individuals and society can influence the behavioural and environmental factors that make such a difference to our chances of ageing well. To do so, we need to move beyond thinking purely in terms of chronological age. For long periods of human history, most people didn't know the date of their birth and weren't numerate or literate enough to calculate their age. As a result, when the Elizabethan Poor Laws were introduced in England in 1601 to provide for the poor and the old, the latter were defined not by their chronological age, which most people didn't know, but by their functional ability: the state of their health and the extent to which they could look after themselves.

It wasn't until the eighteenth century that rising literacy and numeracy ushered in a new era of improved record keeping and policymaking tied to chronological age. School age, marrying age, voting age, and ultimately retirement age all became defined chronologically. It may seem counterintuitive, but the seventeenth-century accent on functional ability is turning into a helpful case study for modern societies. Chronological age is no longer the most reliable guide to increasing longevity. The Elizabethan Poor Laws are resurfacing unexpectedly in the contemporary concept of biological age: in essence, we are as old as our bodies allow us to be.

Recent developments in the biology of ageing have led to the identification of cellular and molecular changes that appear to be hallmarks of the ageing process. These changes impact the functioning of our body, creating the physical and cognitive signs of ageing. Tracking these biological processes raises the prospect of a new measure that may prove more accurate in determining both the quality and quantity of our remaining years.

If we wish to change how we age and ensure we remain healthier for longer, it is biological, not chronological age, that needs to be our focus. Income-driven differences in life expectancy show that how we age is malleable, but developments in the biology of ageing hold out the prospect of treatments and therapeutics that could tackle ageing-related diseases and even ageing itself.

Crucially, the concept of biological age confirms that ageing is not an event – you don't wake up old on your 65th birthday – but a process. This process doesn't start at some undefinable moment when your bones start creaking or you start forgetting where you put your car keys. It begins much earlier in life, perhaps even in utero. The simplest way of putting it: it's never too early to start thinking about longevity.

The implications of an emphasis on biological age are profound, particularly for the health care industry. Not the least reason that life expectancy has increased so dramatically around the globe is that science and medicine have vanquished a wide range of infectious diseases. Smallpox, polio and a wide range of childhood afflictions have been eradicated or largely controlled. As a result, though, a new problem has arisen. Increasing longevity is changing the nature of the world's medical burden from infectious to chronic diseases whose incidence increases with age. The challenges today are diseases that tend to afflict our later years: diabetes, dementia, arthritis and others. Our health systems are beginning to strain under the pressure of treating so many older people with chronic health problems.

Research must, of course, continue into better treatments for sufferers of any disease. But the danger here is that a continuing focus on treatment will produce health systems that keep us alive longer but don't necessarily keep us active longer. If we want to stay healthy for longer – thereby relieving pressure on health care – we need to focus on the process of ageing itself. We need to transform our health care system to prioritise maintaining health rather than treating disease. We need to invest more in preventive measures at an earlier stage so that, at the very least, we can delay the onset of chronic disease.

If we start to think of age as a process, we are well on the way to managing it. Ageing may be inevitable, but you still have a say in how it affects you. Whether it be through so-called 'lifestyle hacks' such as fasting and cryotherapy, traditional remedies like sleep, exercise, abstinence from tobacco or alcohol, or the beguiling prospect of a new class of anti-ageing drugs (yet to be approved or perhaps still waiting to be discovered), the point is that you need not fear longevity.

There's another measure of our age that is also crucial for us to focus on. That measure doesn't focus on how old your body is or how it feels, but on how many years you have left. Economists call it your 'prospective' age. Chronological age focuses on how many years since you were born but what if we look at it the other way round? We might say that old age starts when we are down to our last ten years of life. In Britain, that final decade would have begun, on average, at the age of 68 in 1922; at 72 in 1965 and at 79 today. From this perspective we really are younger for longer.

From an economic point of view, prospective age is an essential driver of behaviour. If my life expectancy is five years longer than my father's, for example, then I will need to invest more for my longer future. I need to think about my health, my finances and my relationships. I need to be sure I'll be able to afford the lifestyle I'd like to enjoy in my eighties or even my nineties and that I will have the health and friendships to achieve it. Thinking in terms of prospective age helps focus on the really important change we face – increasing life expectancy means we have more years ahead of us than past generations. In a profound way, 60 is the new 60.

For most of the twentieth century, life expectancy increased, but the chronological re-tirement age remained unchanged. The inevita-ble result was the addition of several more years of leisure at the end of life. For some, that was doubtless welcome. For others, those years may have proved empty and unrewarding.

But what if we rethought the traditional calendar of our lives? Instead of accumulating extra years at the very end, what if we break up the standard three-stage life course of education, work and retirement? Why don't we take those extra longevity years and, instead of waiting until we're too old to enjoy them, spread them across our lifespan, extending the first two stages and incorporating gap years at opportune moments?

The life course is already being reshaped in response to longevity and of course other factors. Many people already stay in education longer, whether it's four-year degree courses instead of three-year ones or additional years spent on pro-fessional qualifications. Parents are starting families later, with the average age of first marriage for women rising from 24 in 1990 to 31.2 today. In the UK, a woman is more likely to give birth aged over 40 than under 20.

Work patterns are changing rapidly. Retirement is shifting from a sudden stop at a predefined age to a more gradual transition. More people are working part time at older ages, reducing their hours rather than stopping abruptly. The concept of 'un-retirement' has become a thing, with older people taking a few years off before returning to work. The three-stage model of life is splintering from the pressure of social experimentation. Should we think, for example, about treating a midlife crisis with a midlife break?

Economists are fond of reminding us that there's no such thing as a free lunch. It is one thing to plan a battery-recharging gap year and quite another to pay for it. The awkward reality of longevity is that living for longer requires working for longer. If your current calculations are based on retiring at 65 and living until 85, what happens if you live to 90? Yet, politicians around the world have learned that raising the retirement age to prevent pensions from running out is a shortcut to worker revolt.

All this helps explain why our ageing society is enveloped in so much economic pessimism. Because so few people in the past had the chance to live to be very old, we have not established the behaviours, policies and institutions focused on keeping us healthy, productive and engaged over a life of ten decades.

From an economic point of view, what we need is to invest in human capital – that is our education, skills and health – at older ages. Crucially, investing in later-life human capital isn't the same thing as governments just responding by increasing the retirement age. Today, over 80 per cent of 50-year-olds in the UK are still working, but at age 65 only 40 per cent are still employed. If older workers are to keep earning for longer, they need an education system that provides lifelong learning and doesn't just focus on the young. They need a health service focused on prevention rather than treatment. They need more flexible working patterns adapted for older workers. They need firms that don't pursue ageist recruitment policies. This is how we turn the negative economic pessimism of an ageing society into a more positive economic longevity dividend.

The task ahead is daunting. Individuals and society at large are embarking on a radical new chapter in the human experience, focused on transforming the way we age. Ahead of us lies a fundamental redesign of cultural attitudes and multiple social institutions. The scope of the required change is beyond what we as individuals alone can create. Further, rising inequality in how we age also points to the importance of government support of later-life human capital so a long, healthy and engaged life is broadly based and not just the preserve of the wealthy.

But despite the scale of the required systemic change there is still plenty that any individual can achieve, with or without institutional support.

First, the concepts of biological and prospective age need to be embedded in everyone's plan for a long, healthy and happy life. Enjoy your birthdays as you have before, but remember that you exert a significant influence on your own biological age. And it is biological, not chronological age that will make your longevity a reward, not a punishment.

Consider, too, your prospective age. You are not your parents or your grandparents: you may have much more time ahead of you. You need to think differently about how to fill that time. You need to think outside that 'three life stages' box.

The most important thing is not to underestimate the capacity of older people, or your own later years. In other words, don't be ageist. If you underestimate the abilities of older people, then you ignore the potential of the fastest-growing part of the population. And you are ignoring the potential of your own future self. Longer lives mean you can expect to experience a lot more future selves and it is important you become a friend to them.

Past generations could be surprised if they lived long enough to reach their nineties. That is no longer the case, which is why we need to rethink ageing. A first longevity revolution has come to an end – the majority can now expect to become the very old. A second longevity revolution needs to begin, focused on changing how we age. How prepared will you be?

Dare We Grow Old?

by **Vicky Spratt**

Recently, I have found myself wondering more than once whether to stop dying my hair. And, to paraphrase the great American writer Nora Ephron, perhaps ceasing to worry about the appearance of grey hairs, and thereby no longer spending a small fortune on grey avoidance, might be a seldom-acknowledged upside to approaching 40.

And yet last week I found myself sitting in a salon chair for hours while my hair underwent yet another 'transformation' as it might be called in a women's lifestyle magazine.

A few days later, for work reasons, it was necessary that I disclose my age to a colleague. I registered her shock when I said 'thirty-seven'.

'No way,' she said, in genuine surprise. 'I would have said twenty-eight max.'

Briefly, I felt my brain nearly trip up and fall through the trap door laid out before us all: I almost relished being mistaken for a younger woman, practically began to congratulate myself on a whole manner of things: my genetics, good luck, diet, serum regime, Botox doctor, hair choices. Then, I righted myself. The quest for youth is appealing, but ultimately, it is a folly.

Ageing and its symptoms are among life's more predictable occurrences, yet they are also happenings that we prefer to ignore and, increasingly, conceal. Fine lines creeping around your mouth? There's a laser for that. A hint of a furrow between your eyebrows? Freeze them with a shot or two of botulinum toxin. Fear you've left it 'too late' to have children? Inject strong hormones and put some eggs on ice. Worried about your mortality? Engage with conversations about 'longevity' and shovel supplements into your mouth until you rattle when you walk, and you might just stand a chance at cheating death.

It is a strange paradox of human existence that we refuse to acknowledge, let alone accept, one of the few certain trajectories in our lives: that we are born, grow, age, and, ultimately, die.

If secular Western society has anything close to a religion, it is surely the idolatry of youth. The median age of the fashion models who stalk catwalks in London, Paris, Milan and New York, all with the aim of selling the rest of us an aspirational vision, is 23 years old.[34] And, while the average age for lead actors in Hollywood films has risen steadily from mid- to late-30s in the 1980s to 44.7 years old in 2023, it remains true that we simply do not see as many older people on the big screen as would reflect our ageing society.[35]

There is much to recommend being young:

freedom, energy, the ability to see everything with fresh eyes. For that reason, there is also much to recommend listening to the young and giving them space and power to run with new ways of seeing and being. But a careful balance must be struck between empowering and enabling future generations and risking foolish worship of youth at the expense of valuing the wisdom and knowledge which, so often, can only be earned through living.

More of us are older than ever before. Across the globe, we are living longer. And, researchers who have studied global life expectancies say, we 'still haven't reached a biological ceiling for longevity' because so many of the risk factors for death – diet and disease – are still being addressed and countered.[36]

As William Kole noted in his book *The Big 100: The New World of Super-Ageing*, by 2050, the number of people living to 100 years old is projected to increase by eight times to 3.7 million people. That is roughly equivalent to a population the same size as the city of Los Angeles.[37]

And, yet, in spite of what many would see as 'advances' in human life expectancies, our obsession with youth, with slowing the process of ageing and masking its signs speaks to an uncom-

                          Dare We Grow Old?

fortable logic: British society still does not support people in ageing well, let alone living well in older age.

So many of us are in denial about the certainty of our own mortality. I often think of a young woman I met in the North-West of England. She was struggling to make ends meet after a back injury meant she could no longer work her zero hours job in a care home. Barely in her mid-thirties, she was relying on the charity of a Multibank (that's like a foodbank, but it's backed by former Prime Minister Gordon Brown, and you can get anything there from cooking appliances to children's toys), and yet, she felt she had to maintain her lip filler.

Some may read that and immediately feel moved to judge this person. But I put it to you, in a world where precarity is on the rise, for the young as well as the old, can you blame her for not wanting to grow any older? Shame her for wanting to maintain, at least, the appearance of youth, even if, in reality, she had left school, started work and managed to accrue no wealth whatsoever leaving her vulnerable even in early middle age? Far from berating her, I struggle to imagine how she could do anything else.

I often turn the irony of this young woman's situation over in my mind. She was young but seriously injured. The injury had occurred while working in a care home, serious and physically demanding work; poorly paid and fundamentally insecure work. She became injured while caring for older people and, as a result, been forced to stop work and experience how easily anyone – young or old – can slip through the holes in Britain's fraying social security safety net.

Indeed, the more I think about my young woman interviewee, the more I think that trying to find the money to pay for lip filler when you're down and out is an entirely rational response to a society that tells you constantly that you are safer and more valuable as a young person. Particularly, as a young woman.

Time is the particular enemy of women. It marches on and, as it does, supposedly takes so much with it: our 'looks', our fertility, our cultural relevance. We know that older women are underemployed, despite many of them wanting to work. And, added to that, age discrimination is far more commonly reported by women over the age of 50 than it is by men.[38]

There is a fragility to human life that the 'anti-ageing' industry encourages us to ignore, and their marketing is very effective. But the companies and individuals who push products intended to obscure or 'delay' ageing – whether that is filler or collagen supplements – are also in the business of appearances, not reality.

A 50-year-old person with Botox is still 50 years old. A 70-year-old, like Kardashian matriarch Kris Jenner, with a fresh facelift, is still 70 years old. A physically fit 89-year-old who travels to India every winter to do yoga is still 89.

Never before have we so easily been able to alter our physical appearances to give the illusion of youth. And, I wonder, if part of that is because we've never before been so uncomfortable with our mortality in many Western countries? We may be living longer but I question whether we are living well.

You can live an entire life without ever seriously believing that you will age and die. Many people do. And it's easy to understand why. To engage, to properly engage, with ageing forces us to abandon the youthful and naive belief that growing old is something that happens to other people. It is also to face, head on, the certainty of illness, of decline and of death.

Even though half of all five-year-olds alive at this very moment will live to 100 years old and beyond, the inescapable nature of human life is that it is finite: we will all eventually die. Just as the leaves turn yellow, red and brown each year and fall. Just as day turns to night. Just as flowers bloom and wilt. Our corporality is impermanent, our existence transient.

That, really, is why it is so important that we get better at ageing.

Though humans are living longer than at any point in history, not all of us are growing old with equal access to the resources that afford a good life in old age, let alone a good death. And, if what I have seen while travelling around Britain, reporting on inequality in recent years, is anything to go by, that is only going to get worse for those very same future generations who can expect to live far longer than their forebears.

As things stand in Britain, one in five people of State Pension age, that's 65 and older, live in poverty.[39] The Centre for Ageing Better has also warned that older people's prospects have worsened in this country. That includes everything from their finances to social connections and the quality of jobs available to them. Older people from Black, Asian and Minority Ethnic (BAME) backgrounds face even more disadvantaged outcomes because the income and homeownership levels that they start with are lower in comparison to their white peers. This means they face even less stability in older age.

All told, we know that many of today's 20-, 30- and 40-something young adults will be renting their homes from a private landlord forever because homeownership is so expensive and out of reach. This, as several charity executives have lamented to me privately, is a 'ticking time bomb' for Britain's adult social care system, which still relies on the idea that a substantial number of older people will have assets in the form of valuable homes they can sell to fund their care in order to prevent the entire system collapsing under the weight of those who qualify for state support.

The data signs are already flashing red. According to the English Housing Survey, 6 per cent of households headed up by someone who is over 65 years old are currently privately renting.[40] That is a small but significant number. One that the Pensions Policy Institute (PPI) forecasts to nearly treble to 17 per cent by 2040. This matters. We know that private renters have worse health outcomes than homeowners, and, significantly, a growing number of older people will be exposed to that.

We also know that young adults today will retire far later, like in their 70s. In the meantime, we are living reasonably financially precarious lives – in part due to lower homeownership rates but, even for homeowners, because of more expensive mortgages.

In its 2024 report, *Precautionary Tales*, independent think tank Resolution Foundation warned that low savings among British households could present a big social and fiscal problem.[41] It warned that families in the UK were being confronted with a 'triple savings challenge'. This consists of a lack of accessible 'rainy day' savings to cushion small cashflow shocks, inadequate precautionary savings to see people through large and unexpected income shocks, and insufficient savings to provide an adequate income in retirement.

Changes to working life, society and retirement are reshaping temporalities of ageing. But we also have an opportunity to reshape things for the better. Truly secure housing, where we do not live out our days in isolation, would be a particularly good place to start. Britain is unlike other European countries because, even though we are living longer here, we are not necessarily in better health. We must build communities where it's possible to improve that. The solutions are mind-blowingly simple – eating healthily, walking as much as possible, and, crucially, being around people.

Far from fearing or trying to delay ageing, we can embrace and plan for it. I believe that growing old, living through each year of your life and taking stock of what happens is one of the few concrete ways that humans can truly measure anything. With age comes perspective and, with perspective, comes wisdom.

But that wisdom cannot properly be appreciated, let alone harnessed, if we do not set people up to age well. If we did, perhaps we would be less afraid of and determined to conceal our own age. Perhaps we would truly dare to grow old.

Ageing Across the Globe

by **Sweta Rajan-Rankin**

At every stage of our life, we are cared for or care for others. It is an essential part of our human ecology and vital to our survival. As we grow older, care is deeply woven with our experience of ageing. Care can mean many things – love, emotional support, belonging, intimacy. It can also involve physical labour including personal and social care. As the world becomes more global, the ways in which care is provided becomes increasingly disjointed. Rapid population ageing and migration have been the two biggest demographic changes in the last fifty years, and they are changing the way people age, where they age, and the care needs and networks of care that emerge to meet these needs. Where in the past, it may have been more common to age 'in place' (in other words in one's own home country or place of domicile), more and more, ageing elders live away from their families, and are cared for by mostly migrant care workers. As a social worker and a sociologist, I have puzzled over the global dynamics of ageing and care and how we are all connected through it. I explore this through these interconnected stories of real people (pseudonyms used) who are part of a global care chain. These stories are but a microcosm of such occurrences that take place, every day, all over the world.

05:25. Dharavi, Mumbai – Asia's largest slum

Meera (6) and Lalit (5) wake up groggy, ushered by their uncle to leave the house while the rest of the family are asleep. They carry large jute bags and wear thin chappals on their feet. No time to wash or have breakfast, that will come later. Now they must seek the gold within a pile of rubbish.

Every Mumbaikar (Mumbai local) knows Dharavi. A bustling mess of poverty, landfills and some of the most magnificent trading in second-hand leather and luxury goods known to mankind. This resilient and monolithic sprawling settlement stands defiantly against the stark and sharp angles of Mumbai's elite corporate buildings. Many have tried to tame it, but all have failed. Inside is an organised army of informal economy workers, whose labour is the lifeblood of the city. Over twenty years ago, as a student social worker working in the centre of Dharavi, I witnessed countless stories like Meera and Lalit's, members of the rag picker communities, who literally turn the waste of others into monetised value.

07:00. Bandra, a wealthy suburb in Mumbai

'What do you mean you can't come today?' asks Sheila angrily, staring at her dirty kitchen and the uncollected bins.

'Maaf karna didi, meri saasun maan ko bahut dikkat hain. Woh buddhe hain, mujhe gaon jaana padega,' pleads Kamini. ('Forgive me sister, my mother-in-law is in grave trouble, she is very old, and I must return to the village to be with her.')

Kamini is 39, and is the grandmother of Meera and Lalit. She was married at 15. Her daughter is a council worker and her son-in-law is a rickshaw driver. They work even longer hours than her but earn very little to support their family of six. Meera and Lalit are only staying with their uncle in Dharavi for a week; they normally stay with Kamini while they attend school. Kamini must now juggle between caring for her grandchildren, looking after her elderly in-laws, and doing her paid work as a domestic help. However, she has accumulated a lot of goodwill from being one of the best *baiis* in Bandra, one of Mumbai's most elite neighbourhoods. She will ask for this time off because she must; and as the families that depend on her know her worth, they will grumble, but they will acquiesce.

02:30. Hounslow Urgent Care Centre, London

Savitri, senior nurse, yawns and stretches without taking her eyes off the monitor. She's 36 years old. In these early hours, her thoughts turn to her own children, a universe away, in the care of her mother in Kerala, India. It has been two years since she has seen them. The patient in bed seven – an elderly white woman – had come into hospital in a bad way; the notes made clear she'd had a severe stroke. The next few hours would be critical. Savitri wipes the sleep from her eyes, and stares intently at the monitors. No change. She notes this down. And sits down for the big wait that is social care on the front lines.

8:00. Mumbai

Sheila listens to the hold music for the hundredth time, her nails bitten almost to the quick. She has been desperately trying to contact the hospital to enquire about the health of her Scottish mother-in-law who has had a stroke. Nothing, just infernal music. 'Please hold, your call is important to us.' Sheila holds, her hands clasped tightly around the phone, 4,500 miles away, willing the call to be answered.

03:30. Stroke and Rehabilitation Unit, Hounslow, London

'Can we please enquire about Mrs McDonald?' asks Sheila, clutching her husband's hand. 'I am her daughter-in-law, and I'm here with my husband, Robert. My mother-in-law is alone in England; we normally care for her, but we are on a work trip in India.' Robert, white-knuckled and crying, nods.

Savitri replies, 'Hello, miss. I am the senior ward nurse. I am so sorry to tell you, miss ... but your mother-in-law has had a stroke. I know this is upsetting ... please don't cry ... I will look after her like my own mother. She is in safe hands.'

Fifteen minutes later, Savitri's long night shift has come to an end. She taps her phone eagerly, checking the World Clock feature – yes! There is still time. She calls her nephew in Trichur.

'Nephew, quickly! There is a short window before it's school time.'

Selvan, 14, is charged with jumping on his father's LML Vespa, holding the precious parcel in his cloth bag. He bangs on the door of his grandmother's house, one mile down from his own house in the village.

'*Paati*, it is Savitri! I have brought the iPad!' The cloth satchel is unfolded reverentially, and the iPad connected to the internet using Selvan's hotspot mobile 3G network.

'*Amma*! Can I see the girls?' All the fatigue of the past night disappears. Savitri is reunited with her little girls before they go to school. Her own mother is their primary caregiver, as Savitri now cares for someone else's mother, so she can support her family, and finally come home.

Conversations like these are taking place every day: across different time zones, countries and continents. I've seen and studied them, and they show us the wide-ranging networks of care that underpin how people age and are cared for as they age, at every stage of life. From the slums of Mumbai to the NHS stroke wards in London, there is an army of informal and formal workers involved in the essential service of social care. Where a vacuum is created in the care chain, another person steps in to fill the gap. These chains of care, provided almost exclusively by women, are often invisible, but they connect the way people age across the globe.

The term 'global care chains'[42] refers to 'a series of personal links between people across the globe based on the paid or unpaid work of caring'. This network of labour is a vital way by which the global ecosystem of caring is sustained. We met Mrs McDonald in London, whose provision of elder care includes many links of informal and formal arrangements. By working as a stroke rehabilitation nurse providing care for Mrs McDonald, Savitri has had to leave her own children in the care of her mother in a village in Kerala. Further down the care chain, Mrs McDonald's daughter-in-law Sheila, who has been providing informal care for her, is herself dependent on the domestic help of her maid Kamini, who in turn has her own family care commitments for her grandchildren and elderly parents. These stories are playing out across the world every day: networks of care communities connecting very different people, and shaping what it means to grow older and be cared for.

These global care chains may have intensified with global capitalism, but they are by no means new. In colonial India for example, as early as 1777, a new servile class emerged in the form of domestic servants, local women called Ayahs who were charged with childcare, upholding European standards of cleanliness and domestic management of the household. Highly skilled workers, Ayahs were cultural border-crossers, navigating between their own cultural backgrounds and the norms and expectations of English culture. Intimately entangled within the English household, but not on equal terms, Indian Ayahs were among the first Indian migrants to cross the seas and travel to England with their colonial employers. It is important to recognise the unequal terms under which Ayahs performed their duties. Archival records show that these Indian Ayahs, whose role was somewhere between servant and surrogate mother, were often taken by the colonising families to England only to be abandoned after arrival. Care networks have always been gendered and racialised.[43]

In the past few decades, global ageing has also been shaped by environmental factors such as climate change and migration. With rapid globalisation, more and more workers are migrating from the global South to North America, the UK and Europe. When workers migrate, they often end up raising their families away from their homelands, which can create a care crisis. Younger couples struggle to juggle childcare with work, while elderly parents struggle without their children's care back home. And yet networks of care are resilient, and migrant families have sometimes found novel solutions to meet these missing links in the care chain. Elderly relatives often visit their adult children for extended periods of time, often for as long as six months to a year, to provide care in the host country. This solves geographical problems for adult children, who can then also care for their elderly parents in their own homes abroad.

But what happens to elderly parents who can't afford or are not well enough to travel? Sometimes nuclear families opt out of caring in person for their elders, providing financial support instead. Ageing in place comes with its own challenges, including loneliness and social isolation. From retirement villages to laughing clubs, elderly people who can afford to stay in semi-independent care homes can enjoy community living with many social and leisure activities. A particularly novel solution in India to address social isolation among the elderly comes from the 'Son for Hire' enterprise, where older women can contact a service to employ a younger man to accompany her to social events such as weddings and community gatherings. If her own son is thousands of miles away, through this be-

                              Ageing Across the Globe

friending service she can find a temporary son, so she can maintain her social networks with a friendly face by her side.

Increasingly, the rising cost of health and social care and long waiting times have led to frustrated older people seeking private social care in warmer locales at a fraction of the cost, upending the usual movement of people from the global South to the global North. In the popular film *The Best Exotic Marigold Hotel*, Dev Patel plays a charming entrepreneurial Indian man who runs a hotel for elderly Western clients. Here, the monetisation of cultural stereotypes of Southern hospitality, geniality and service helps to create a private social care industry reminiscent of the colonial past, but through the newer guise of health and social care tourism.

Ageing is an inevitable part of the human condition and brings with it different needs for care across the life course. When global migration is added to the mix, new dynamics of ageing come to life, with greater crossover between paid and informal care, the cared for, and those who provide care (who are increasingly migrant workers from the global South). There are many assumptions about care – for instance, social discourses that dictate that families should provide care for their elderly and that it is a duty performed out of love. And yet, these networks of care show us that both informal and formal care are ordered in much more complex ways that involve marketising the principles of love while providing them through surrogate migrant labour. Care provision is unequally ordered, with a greater proportion of migrant workers from the global South providing the care, and the cared-for population originating from or residing in the global North. Global care chains, these invisible networks of care that span the globe, make clear to us that care provision is a classed, gendered and racialised form of labour. It is one that we must pay attention to, as we are all connected to or affected by it, in one way or another.

Disability, and Other Denials

by **Tom Shakespeare**

On his 75th birthday, I rang a family friend to congratulate him.

'Happy birthday!' I said cheerfully.

'What do you mean, "happy"?' he replied, somewhat like Eeyore. 'There's nothing happy about getting older.'

'Doesn't it get easier?'

'No.'

I was disheartened. I'd assumed at some point we come to terms with growing older. It seemed for my friend, and for many of us, the regular reminder of our mortality with another birthday doesn't get better.

But what lies at the heart of this fear?

When we grow older, inevitably we lose some of our powers, and often encounter frailty somewhere along the way. Disabled people might be able to help here. From my perspective, I often see a denial of disability by older people, or a desire to mask or make up for any weakness. In my experience, the part of ageing that many people feel most worried about is dependency, and with it issues such as mobility and dexterity, and memory.

People have always thought of themselves as 'hale and hearty'. Independent. Now with the passage of time, they come to know that they aren't: they might get tired quicker, forget things, struggle with tasks that they used to be able to do. Any social gathering of 50- or 60-somethings seems to be a case of people listing their aches and pains, and complaining about their teeth and their eyesight. As Hamlet says, 'the thousand natural shocks that flesh is heir to'.

Disabled people have usually got here first, and we are here to say: you can do it! You can come to terms with life's inevitable restrictions, and you are no less of a person if you cannot do it all. There is no need for disability denial. That is, you can lead a happy and fulfilled existence even if you have less strength, even if you are blind, even if you are deaf, even if you are paralysed, even if you have dementia.

I say this as someone who grew up with restricted growth, who became paraplegic over about three days at the age of 42.

Like anyone who has such an immense life change, it was hard to come to terms with. When it first happened, I wanted to die, because I thought life was over for me. Thankfully, it wasn't. It turned out, many of the most exciting things in my life were ahead of me, not behind me.

True, I had to relearn to navigate the world with a totally new disability, having now become a wheelchair user. I also had to learn about bow-el and bladder management, about protecting skin and the avoidance of pressure sores. I also had to spend many hours with physiotherapists and wheelchair technicians. When you are in a wheelchair, you learn how dependent you are on assistance from others, particularly if your job involves travel. And if you have an incomplete spinal cord injury, you have to learn about neu-ropathic pain, which will afflict you for the rest of your days, and often wake you up in the night as well. And if you can come to terms with that, you can come to terms with almost anything.

Becoming paraplegic was not all bad: peo-ple stare at wheelchair users a lot less than they stare at restricted growth folks. It was almost as if the wheelchair was my invisibility cloak. Peo-ple are more likely to write off and ignore peo-ple who use wheelchairs, not goggle at them. Which is certainly awful, but not as hard as being thought of as odd and inherently entertaining, which is often the experience of those with re-stricted growth or other visible differences.

Here, I want to make a distinction, which at first sounds like a paradox. Disability is often neg-ative, but life with a disability is usually positive. People do not generally welcome being unable

                    Disability, and Other Denials

to do things. Nobody wants a disability. But they find that afterwards they adapt well to almost everything, and life goes on. There are usually other things to worry about. The evidence shows that quality of life of disabled people is often as good as that of non-disabled people. Which of course is good news.

People may think that disability will never happen to them. But the chances are, it will, and if not directly, then via a family member or loved one. At least 16 per cent of people are disabled: there is a strong age gradient, and half of all disabled people are over 60. Some people will only encounter serious illness and impairment when they reach old age. It may be unfamiliar to them. Others will have lived as disabled people for many decades. They may have developed MS or a spinal cord injury in midlife. They may have been disabled children with autism or muscular dystrophy. Or they may have been born with dwarfism or Down syndrome. If you have been disabled all your life, you will have got used to being different. And remember, 40 per cent of people who receive social care support are in this category. Disability may well be part of your identity.

If it is a new development, it may be a

shock. After all, you have been non-disabled all your life. Being non-disabled is probably part of your identity. You have become the other, the one you always felt sorry for. You are used to being a man or a woman, to your sexuality, your ethnicity, but not to being disabled. And you may not like it.

For many older people, the aim seems to be to pretend not to be disabled for as long as possible. 'This is normal ageing,' they might say. 'Don't call me disabled.' But are those spectacles, that hearing aid, and this stick really badges of age, not disability? I think the sooner you consider yourself a disabled person, the easier life will be. The only answer to living a full life with disability is to embrace it, not deny it.

I wondered to what extent this aversion to disability among older people was culturally specific to Britain. Then I met a researcher from Uganda who said she had often encountered this reluctance or denial in her research with older people. Maybe it is worldwide.

How can we change the narrative? How do we dismantle the stigma attached to ageing, and attached to disabled people? Many traditional societies seem to venerate elders, and of course for them disability would be more common and

                    Disability, and Other Denials

more familiar. I think the way forward for all of us, whatever life stage we are at, is not to think of disability as a disaster.

Disability, at any age, is part of life, not a failure. It just is – and it's normal. Some of us live good lives without important human powers, like sight or hearing or mobility. We are all frail human beings, and the sooner we accept that, the better. We are all vulnerable to temporary or permanent disability, and we are all mortal. There's no need for denial of either reality. I do not believe we will ever eliminate disability. It is part of life. Prehistoric burials show it has been with us from the birth of humanity, and although its impact may be much reduced with technology and health care advances, I do not think it will ever be ended entirely, any more than I think we will live lifespans much beyond what the luckiest of us achieve now. We know we have to come to terms with mortality; I think we also have to come to terms with disability, as part of this reckoning.

Those of us who have experienced disability for years have had to learn how to cope with limitation, with experiencing barriers, with other people's reactions. We can joke about disability – the stupidities and the disasters. We may use Braille. We may communicate using British

Sign Language. We realise that disability does not mean the end of sex. We might know how to get a wheelchair into a car. We know who to call. We know how to ask for the support we need.

I hear from people in my parents' generation who do not like using the assisted technology that many of us have relied on for years: the wheelchairs and shower chairs, the hearing aids, the glasses. But these aids are not admissions of defeat, they are assistive technologies which make life so much easier.

And not just those: all the gadgets which exist and can make life more convenient, like hand-held vacuum cleaners, and audiobooks, and e-readers. Many of these everyday technologies began as adaptions for disabled communities – before being embraced by the mainstream. Access is good for everyone, in the end. I used to feel awful about the number of things I forgot, until somebody showed me how to set reminders in my phone, and now life is unthinkable without them. I felt ashamed of needing a reminder, until she said that everyone does it, these days: there's no need for denial. It's not an admission of a failing memory, it is a response to a busy schedule. As another friend of mine says, her mind is like an overflowing sieve: so

Disability, and Other Denials

many things to remember, and forget.

Assisted technology is stigmatised when associated with disability, because it seems like an admission of failure. My grandfather used to have bulky taped books, when his failing eyesight meant that he could read for himself no longer. But now people who are working out, or ironing, or walking the dog, listen to their literature via Audible or another source of audiobooks, and feel no shame about it. There is no longer any stigma associated with audiobooks, now they have become ubiquitous.

Because it is really only stigma and bad planning which stops people using what could make their life so much better. I wish, as they age, people would learn from disabled people. For example, why don't people have better accessibility in their homes? If they were to buy or rent a home on flat ground; if they were to avoid many steps to the property; ensure the dwelling has a downstairs loo, or better still a shower room. Suddenly, I can visit them, notwithstanding my wheelchair, and more importantly, they can age in place, rather than having to move house, or go into a care home.

Of course, accessibility may be impossible in a private rented dwelling. But it is possible for the 65 per cent of the British population who own their homes, and it should also be possible for those who live in social housing (17 per cent of people in England), if housing associations and local authorities take disability and ageing seriously. That would ideally mean building in accessibility from the beginning, as with the Lifetime Homes concept, not retrofitting.

When I became suddenly paralysed in 2008, I spent a total of ten weeks in rehabilitation in North-East England. I was on a ward with a man who had been rolled over by a horse, a man who had fallen from a mountain bike and a teen who had been trying to jump a quad bike. Like me, they were all now paralysed. But I was the only one who could go home after my rehabilitation was complete, because my home was already wheelchair-friendly: I lived in a bungalow and had a wet room. Everyone was desperate to get out, but only I could, because I was the only one who had an accessible house.

Other disability innovations are less obvious. For example, we have challenged the connection between physical dependency and social dependency. What matters is not doing it, but having choice and agency over how it is done. Think about hot drinks: what matters is being

 Disability, and Other Denials

able to ask for a tea with milk but no sugar. Or a coffee with two sweeteners. Or a shower this morning instead of a bath last night, or toast for breakfast. What matters is to feel in control.

This is the philosophy of independent living, as created by disabled people in the US and the UK and adopted worldwide. Often, it is associated with another innovation, the personal assistant (PA). They are paid a wage for doing things that may be physically difficult or impossible, such as cooking or driving.

Supermarkets have delivered for decades, to anyone who can access them on the internet. You can go online for some retail therapy, and issue polite requests for what you want, assuming you have money for that. And everything is delivered by those friendly drivers who seem to deliver everything we need these days. We live in a world where not being able to shop, or to carry heavy bags, need not be a problem for anyone. That's good for disabled people like me, as it is for many older people.

As the following example shows, the environment you live in can make you more dependent or less dependent. When I was first disabled, I needed a PA to get me into the building where I was living while I worked in Geneva. It was an old town house, and I could not reach the keyhole. Then I moved to a more accessible home and I have not needed a PA since. If I could not reach things in the kitchen or bathroom, I might need one. But I have the resources to set up my environment for me. That might mean a helping-hand helper for when I need to pick things up, or what I call my pokey-pokey stick (a length of dowel with a rubber ferrule on the end) for when I cannot reach the switch, or it might mean a more accessible bathroom and kitchen.

These assistive technologies might be cognitive, not physical. For example, I write things down on a whiteboard in my hall, so I do not forget them. I have mentioned alerts in my phone, which now warn me when afternoon events are about to start. All this helps me age with the inattentions of ADHD.

The place which you call home can also make it more possible for you to live independently. I live in an ex-council block of flats. I know my neighbours on both sides, who I can ask to change my light bulb, or reach me down another jar of marmalade, or even change the wheel on my assistive device. A sense of community means that you look out for each other. In return, I give a cup of coffee or a glass of wine.

Others might feed the cat, or child-sit a sleeping toddler – communities are useful at every stage of life. But it is particularly useful for disabled people if others can spend five minutes doing the tasks – like changing the light bulb or reaching down the food mixer – which have eluded them.

For a community to be useful in this way, people need to stop and say hello, not walk past and ignore. Everyone needs to sign up to a list for the building or street, probably online. The WhatsApp group (or similar) has made connection so much easier. That's the way you can be part of the street party in the summer, or the gathering to celebrate Christmas or Hannukah or Eid, if you want to. Disabled or older people might not be isolated or forgotten. Of course, it's easier to build community where a gate or an entrance is shared; harder where each lives in their own detached house; more difficult when people are so exhausted from work that they have no time for themselves, let alone their neighbour. Some communities are stronger than others, perhaps because they have more time, less precarious income, more social entrepreneurs.

I would prefer not to speak of independent living, a phrase that is often used by the disability movement, because no one is truly independent.

We all need each other, young and old. Children need parents, parents need children, neighbours need each other. Let's think of community living, as opposed to residential care; a way of life that helps us live longer in our own homes. Or even better, integrated living, because shouldn't we be connected to each other?

But maybe it is not physical dependency which is frightening. Perhaps it is psychological dependency, confusion and dementia. I was once as frightened by dementia as anyone. After all, my brain is my tool when it comes to writing and talking. But then I met lots of people with dementia, through the DEEP network, and realised that my fear of dementia was mostly another form of stigma.

Because disability rights principles got here first too. First, let's not get hung up on the medical diagnosis. Second, let's not go immediately to the worst possible outcome. The diagnosis usually comes before the condition develops. Above all, let's remember the person. They may begin to forget things, or need simpler phones and regular reminders, but that's fine. They are still the same person, and still have the same human rights. Let's connect people through their computers or phones. Let's organise the context

                    Disability, and Other Denials

so it is not more disabling than it need be. Let's make the city age-friendly.

If we are lucky, ageing will come to us all. After all, death is far worse than disability, however you may think in the spur of the moment. After all, we all need each other, and we all rely on our gadgets. 'Nothing about us, without us' can help with making it all easier. Assistive technologies, accessibility and reasonable accommodation are often the practical answer. Many of us have been solving these problems all our lives. There are so many ways to make ageing easier and less frightening. Most of them start from listening to people directly affected. Why not learn from fifty years of disability inclusion?

I hope, by the time I reach 75 myself, I will have come to terms with death. Mortality is a different matter from increasing levels of disability, and much harder. As I learned from my older friend, it doesn't necessarily get any easier when it is staring you in the face.

That's why, when I turned 35, I invited people to a 'halfway' party. When my friends opened the invitation, they found this quotation from John Donne:

We are all conceived in close prison; in our mothers' wombs, we are close prisoners all; when we are born, we are born but to the liberty of the house; prisoners still, though within larger walls: and then all our life is but a going out to the place of execution, to death. Now was there ever any man seen to sleep in the cart, between Newgate, and Tyburn? Between the prison, and the place of execution, does any man sleep? And we sleep all the way; from the womb to the grave we are never thoroughly awake ...

'Wake up,' I said to them in 2001, and say now to you.

                    Disability, and Other Denials

Endnotes

1   The braided wick folded as it burned, replacing the simpler twisted
    wick, which required regular trimming.

2   Pat Thane, ed., A History of Old Age (London: Thames & Hudson,
    2005), 9. Thane estimates that around 10 per cent of the European
    population were aged 60 or over by the eighteenth century.

3   This quotation does not appear in any poem by Robert Frost but has
    been widely attributed to him. Whatever its origin, it expresses a
    relationship to ageing rather nicely.

4   See, for example, Megan Brickley, Adrian Miles and Hilary Stainer,
    The Cross Bones Burial Ground, Redcross Way, Southwark,
    London: Archaeological Excavations (1991–1998) for the London
    Underground Limited Jubilee Line Extension Project (London:
    MoLAS, 1999). Their excavations revealed a host of musculoskeletal
    and other problems, even in the relatively young.

5   Thane, A History of Old Age, 204.

6   Judith Worsnop, 'A re-evaluation of "the problem of surplus women"
    in 19th-century England: The case of the 1851 census', Women's
    Studies International Forum 13:1–2 (1990), 21–31.

7   'National life tables: Life expectancy in the UK, 2018–2020', Office
    for National Statistics (23 September 2021).

8   Tom Rutherford, 'Population ageing: statistics', researchbriefings.
    files.parliament.uk/documents/SN03228/SN03228.pdf (10
    February 2012). See also: 'Families and households in the UK: 2024',
    Office for National Statistics (23 July 2025).

9   Ursula K. Le Guin, The Wave in the Mind: Talks and Essays on the
    Writer, the Reader, and the Imagination (Boston: Shambhala,
    2004), 142.

10 Kathleen P. Lasher and Patricia J. Faulkender, 'Measurement of
    aging anxiety: Development of the anxiety about aging scale',
    International Journal of Aging and Human Development 37:4
    (1993), 247–59.

11 R. Ng, 'Societal Age Stereotypes in the U.S. and U.K. from a Media Database of 1.1 Billion Words', International Journal of Environmental Research and Public Health 18:16 (2021), 8822.

12 Charlie McCurdy, 'Ageing in the Fast And Slow Lane: Examining Geographic Gaps in Ageing', Resolution Foundation (January 2025).

13 Sarah Fraser et al., 'Ageism and COVID-19: What does our society's response say about us?', Age and Ageing 49:5 (2020), 692–5.

14 This showed the mortality rates to be much lower initially. Later on, a specific reporting process was set up by the French Public Health Agency to tackle this.

15 Fiona Costa, 'The fear of old age: a survey of adults in the UK', Educational Gerontology 51:5 (2025), 532–49.

16 L.B. Anderson and P.E. Gettings, 'Old age scares me: Exploring young adults' feelings about aging before and during COVID-19', Journal of Aging Studies 60 (March 2022).

17 Marie Mazerolle et al., 'Negative aging stereotypes impair performance on brief cognitive tests used to screen for predementia', Journals of Gerontology: Series B 72:6 (2017), 932–6.

18 Waqar Husain et al., 'Gerascophobia or Excessive Fear of Aging Scale (GEFAS): Development, validation, and exploration of psychometric properties of a brief instrument using classical testing theory and item response theory', Archives of Gerontology and Geriatrics 128 (2025).

19 World Population Ageing 2017, United Nations: Department of Economic and Social Affairs (2017).

20 Dr. Aisha Islam and Dr. Ifeoma Offiah, Older Women in the UK: Building a Picture of Older Women's Lives, Age UK (March 2025).

21 HelpAge International, 'Things Have Just Gotten Worse': The Impact of the Global Food, Fuel and Finance Crisis on Older People (April 2023).

22 Claire Samtleben and Kai-Uwe Müller, 'Care and careers: Gender (in)equality in unpaid care, housework and employment', Research in Social Stratification and Mobility 77 (2022).

23 Sara Carmel, 'Health and well-being in late life: Gender differences worldwide', Frontiers in Medicine 6:218 (2019).

24 Malina Bodea and Dr. Miranda Davies, 'Silence, sexism and stigma: The state of working-age women's health in England', Nuffield Trust (2025).

25 Joan Chrisler, Angela Barney and Brigida Palatino, 'Ageism can be hazardous to women's health: Ageism, sexism, and stereotypes of older women in the healthcare system', Journal of Social Issues 72:1 (2016), 86–104.

26 'Ageing', Office for National Statistics, ons.gov.uk/peoplepopulationandcommunity/birthsdeathsandmarriages/ageing.

27 'Map of healthy life expectancy at birth', The Health Foundation (25 February 2025).

28 'Life expectancy for local areas in England, Northern Ireland and Wales: between 2001 to 2003 and 2020 to 2022', Office for National Statistics (26 January 2024).

29 Ben Sanders and Alice Dore, 'I Didn't Expect to Be Living the Way I Am': Older People's Experiences of Housing Precarity and Homelessness, Crisis (August 2025).

30 Chloe Reeves, Dr. Aisha Islam and Tom Gentry, The State of Health and Care of Older People in England 2025, Age UK (September 2025).

31 Zosia Kmietowicz, 'Sixty seconds on … geriatric BMI', British Medical Journal 389:r786 (2025).

32 Ethnic health inequalities in later life: The persistence of disadvantage from 1993-2017, Centre for Ageing Better (November 2021).

33 World Population Ageing 2015, United Nations: Department of Economic and Social Affairs (2015).

34 George Arnett, 'Despite push for age diversity, young models still rule the runway', Vogue Business (17 February 2020).

35 Ben Lindbergh and Rob Arthur, 'The Golden Age of the Aging Actor', The Ringer (27 June 2022).

36 Tom Seymour, 'We are no longer living longer, study shows', University of Exeter News (18 February 2025).

37 William J Kole, 'A "longevity revolution" is coming. Here's how those over 100 are making the most of their lives', The Guardian (28 April 2024).

38 'Many women experience glaring inequalities says new Age UK report', Age UK (10 March 2025).

39 'Inequalities in later life', Centre for Ageing Better, ageing-better. org.uk/inequalities-later-life.

40 'Annex tables for English Housing Survey 2023 to 2024 headline findings on demographics and household resilience', gov.uk (28 November 2024).

41 Molly Broome, Ian Mulheirn and Simon Pittaway, 'Precautionary Tales: Tackling the problem of low saving among UK households', Resolution Foundation (February 2024).

42 Arlie Russell Hochschild, 'Global care chains and emotional surplus value', in Daniel Engster and Tamara Metz (eds), Justice, Politics, and the Family (New York: Routledge, 2014), 249–61.

43 Satya Shikha Chakraborty and Shalini Grover, 'Care-work for colonial and contemporary white families in India: A historical-anthropology of the racialized romanticization of the ayah', Cultural Dynamics 34:4 (2022), 297–319.

About the Authors

Dr. Pragya Agarwal is an interdisciplinary scholar of social inequities and injustice, and founder of a research think tank working at the intersection of geography, sociology and technology. She is the author of *Sway: Unravelling Unconscious Bias*, *(M)otherhood: On the Choices of Being a Woman* and *Hysterical: Exploding the Myth of Gendered Emotions*, among others. She currently teaches at the University of Cambridge and is a visiting professor at Loughborough University.

Travis Alabanza is an award-winning theatre maker and writer. Their plays *Burgerz*, *Overflow* and *Sound of the Underground* have received critical acclaim and toured internationally. Their debut book *None of the Above: Reflections on Life Beyond the Binary* was a Waterstones bestseller, won the Jhalak Literary Prize and was listed as one of *Time* magazine's 'Must Read Books of 2023'.

Dr. Sharon Blackie is the award-winning and bestselling author of seven books, and a psychologist with a background in mythology and folklore. Her work is focused on the relevance of myths and fairy tales to the personal, cultural and environmental issues we face today. She's a Fellow of the Royal Society of Arts and an Honorary Member of the UK Association of Jungian Analysts, and her much-loved publication 'The Art of Enchantment' is a Top Ten Global Literature Substack.

Molly Conisbee is a bereavement counsellor, trainee death doula, and social historian. A visiting research fellow at the Centre for Death and Society at the University of Bath, her book *No Ordinary Deaths: A People's History of Mortality* (Wellcome/Profile) was published in May 2025.

Dr. Sweta Rajan-Rankin is a Reader in Social Work and Sociology at the University of Kent. An arts-based researcher and professional social worker, her research examines the relationship between race, racialisation, ageing and embodiment.

Venki Ramakrishnan won the 2009 Nobel Prize in Chemistry for uncovering the structure of the ribosome. He runs the Ramakrishnan Lab at the MRC Laboratory of Molecular Biology in Cambridge, UK. From 2015 to 2020, he served as president of the Royal Society in London. He is the author of *Gene Machine: The Race to Decipher the Secrets of the Ribosome* and *Why We Die: The New Science of Ageing and Longevity.*

Angela Saini is an assistant professor of science writing at the Massachusetts Institute of Technology, and the author of four books exploring aspects of human difference and inequality. Her most recent, *The Patriarchs: How Men Came to Rule*, was a finalist for the Orwell Prize for Political Writing.

Andrew J. Scott is Professor of Economics at London Business School and Senior Director of Economics at the Ellison Institute of Technology, Oxford. He is the author of *The Longevity Imperative: Building a Better Society for Healthier, Longer Lives* and (with Lynda Gratton) *The 100-Year Life: Living and Working in an Age of Longevity.*

Lynne Segal is Professor Emerita of Gender and Psychosocial Studies, Birkbeck, University of London. She still publishes widely, most recently on feminism, ageing and care. Recent books include *Out of Time: The Pleasures and Perils of Ageing* (2013); *Radical Happiness: Moments of Collective Joy* (2017); *The Care Manifesto* (co-authored with the Care Collective) (2020); and *Lean on Me: A Politics of Radical Care* (2023).

Tom Shakespeare is Professor of Disability Research at the London School of Hygiene and Tropical Medicine. His books include *Disability Rights and Wrongs*, and the novels *The Ha-Ha* and *The Ends*.

Vicky Spratt is an award-winning journalist, author and housing rights advocate. She has been shortlisted for the Orwell Prize three years in a row (2023, 2024, 2025). Her first book, *Tenants: The People on the Frontline of Britain's Housing Emergency*, was a *Financial Times* book of the year in 2022, and her second book, *We Were Promised the Moon*, will be published in 2026.

About the Exhibition

The Coming of Age is a major exhibition at Wellcome Collection (26 March–29 November 2026), curated by Shamita Sharmacharja and Ruth Horry.

Globally people are living longer – one in ten children in the UK can expect to live beyond 100 – yet many face health and social inequalities throughout life that impact older age. The exhibition asks how societies can adapt to ensure everyone ages better.

More than 120 artworks and objects are featured in the exhibition, from Sebald Beham's medieval woodcut depicting elders rejuvenated by the mythical fountain of youth (1536) to 1930s adverts for Kellogg's All-Bran cereal that claim to keep consumers young. Contemporary works range from Deborah Roberts' *King Me* (2019) – a series that highlights the societal challenges that Black children face as they strive to build their identity – to Robert Mapplethorpe's portrait of a playful and defiant 70-year-old Louise Bourgeois, ahead of her first major museum retrospective.

The Coming of Age explores what ageing means for us throughout our lives, and how our experience of age is shaped by our environment, culture and society. By bringing together objects across time and artistic disciplines, the exhibition asks what changes are needed for us all to age better.

wellcome
collection